RECORDING ENGLAND'S PAST

A review of national and local
Sites and Monuments Records
in England

ROYAL COMMISSION ON THE HISTORICAL MONUMENTS OF ENGLAND

Cover pictures (clockwise from top left)

Lanion Quoit, St Just, Cornwall
Earl's Barton church, Northamptonshire
Bronze Age ring ditches, Witchampton, Dorset
Black Pig Inn, Staple, Kent
Roman fort, Chesterholm, Northumberland
Horse Sand Fort, Solent, Hampshire
Water wheel, Lumbhole Mill, Kettleshulme, Cheshire
Iron Age hillfort and medieval castle, The Rings, Loddiswell, Devon

Published by the Royal Commission on the Historical Monuments of England, Fortress House, 23 Savile Row, London W1X 2JQ

©RCHME Crown copyright 1993

First published 1993

ISBN 1 873592 17 5

British Library Cataloguing in Publication Data
A CIP catalogue record for this book is available from the British Library

All rights reserved
No part of this publication may be reproduced, stored in a retrieval system, or transmitted in any form or by any means mechanical, electronic, photocopying, recording or otherwise, without the prior permission of the publisher.

Designed by Chuck Goodwin, 27 Artesian Road, London W2 5DA

Printed by J W Dunn Limited, Kimpton Industrial Estate, Sutton, Surrey SM3 9RS

Contents

Foreword   v
List of abbreviations   vi
Summary of conclusions   vii

■ 1   INTRODUCTION   1

1·1   Scope and purpose of the SMR Review   1
1·2   The development of the national record of archaeological sites and monuments   1
1·3   The development of local records of archaeological sites and monuments   2
1·4   The need for a review of SMRs   3
1·5   Objectives of the SMR Review   4
1·6   Methodology   4

■ 2   THE ROYAL COMMISSION ON THE HISTORICAL MONUMENTS OF ENGLAND AND THE NATIONAL MONUMENTS RECORD   5

2·1   The Royal Commission on the Historical Monuments of England   5
2·2   The National Monuments Record   5
2·3   The National Archaeological Record – core functions and priorities   6
2·4   The National Buildings Record   6
2·5   The National Library of Air Photographs   7
2·6   Computerisation of the NMR   7
2·7   Public access to information in the NMR   9
2·8   Use of the NMR   9
2·9   Use of data in the NMR for RCHME publications   9
2·10   Copyright and charging for information in the NMR   10
2·11   Liaison with SMRs   11
2·12   Information standards work   11
2·13   Costs   12

■ 3   LOCAL SITES AND MONUMENTS RECORDS IN ENGLAND   13

3·1   Introduction   13
3·2   Local Sites and Monuments Records in England – core functions   13
3·3   County and metropolitan SMRs   13
3·4   Staffing levels of county and metropolitan SMRs   14
3·5   District SMRs   15
3·6   National Park SMRs   15
3·7   The National Trust   16
3·8   The Greater London SMR   16
3·9   Computerisation of SMRs   16
3·10   Public access to information in SMRs   19
3·11   Academic research, education and publication   20
3·12   Use of SMRs   21
3·13   Copyright and charging for information in SMRs   23
3·14   Costs   24

■ 4   SCOPE AND CONTENT OF THE NATIONAL AND LOCAL RECORDS   27

4·1   Introduction   27
4·2   The National Archaeological Record: breadth of coverage   27
4·3   The National Archaeological Record: depth of coverage   27
4·4   The National Archaeological Record: current review   28
4·5   The National Archaeological Record: compilation from secondary sources   28
4·6   The National Archaeological Record: compilation from survey and recording   28

4·7	The National Archaeological Record: recording manuals and quality control	29
4·8	The National Archaeological Record: size and reliability	29
4·9	The National Archaeological Record: map-based records	29
4·10	Other related archaeological records held by the RCHME	30
4·11	Sites and Monuments Records: breadth of coverage	30
4·12	Sites and Monuments Records: depth of coverage	31
4·13	Sites and Monuments Records: data standards and structure	31
4·14	Sites and Monuments Records: compilation from secondary sources	31
4·15	Sites and Monuments Records: compilation from primary survey and recording	33
4·16	Recording manuals and quality control	34
4·17	Size and reliability of SMR databases	34
4·18	Map-based records	37
4·19	Other non-computerised records held by SMRs	38
4·20	Updating the National Archaeological Record and Sites and Monuments Records through data exchange	38

5 THE ROLES OF THE NMR AND SMRS 40

5·1	The extended national record	40
5·2	RCHME responsibility for the oversight of local Sites and Monuments Records	40
5·3	Improved liaison procedures	40
5·4	Training and specialist support for SMRs	40
5·5	RCHME support for SMR computer systems	41
5·6	The role of SMRs	41
5·7	Staffing levels of SMRs	42
5·8	The location of SMRs within local authorities	42
5·9	The impartiality of archaeological advice to local authorities	42
5·10	National Parks	43
5·11	District authorities	43
5·12	Historic buildings	43
5·13	The status of SMRs	44
5·14	Local government reorganisation: county, district and National Park SMRs	44
5·15	Greater London SMR	45
5·16	Copyright and charging for information in the NMR and SMRs	45
5·17	Costs of future SMR provision	45

6 THE FUTURE ORGANISATION, SCOPE AND CONTENT OF THE EXTENDED NATIONAL RECORD 47

6·1	The extended national record	47
6·2	Access to the extended national record	47
6·3	NMR responsibility for the enhancement of the extended record	48
6·4	SMR responsibility for the enhancement of the extended record	49
6·5	RCHME support for SMR enhancement	50
6·6	Local authority support for SMR enhancement	50
6·7	Areas for SMR enhancement	50
6·8	RCHME support for data standards work	51
6·9	Standards for cartographic records	51
6·10	Geographic Information Systems	51
6·11	Computer security	52
6·12	Other related archaeological records	52
6·13	Collections of aerial photographs	53

References 54

Foreword

Central government, local authorities and the community are today united in their concern to protect the best of England's unique historic environment. To do so they need an easily accessible inventory of the many thousands of archaeological sites that are now known to lie within and beneath England's cities, towns, villages and countryside.

In recent years, the development of such a record has moved along parallel paths. At the centre, the Royal Commission on the Historical Monuments of England (RCHME) is required by government to maintain a national public record of archaeological sites and historic buildings. At a regional level, more than fifty local authorities have developed their own Sites and Monuments Records (SMRs) to make archaeological information and advice available to the local authority planning system, and to serve the wider needs of conservation, education and research.

In 1989 the government confirmed that the Royal Commission should in future maintain a 'lead role' for SMRs in England, thereby allowing the work of SMRs and its own National Monuments Record (NMR) to be more effectively co-ordinated. On the eve of local government reorganisation, the Royal Commission has accordingly carried out a detailed review of the way in which SMRs and the NMR are currently organised and how they should develop to meet the needs of the future.

Our review concludes that information about archaeological sites and historic buildings must continue to be accessible at both local and national levels. We also argue that records maintained by SMRs, the NMR, English Heritage, the Department of National Heritage and other organisations need to be more closely linked. This is not only to avoid duplication of effort, but to obtain maximum benefit from the power of modern information technology and systems of electronic communication.

Our solution is therefore to recommend that the record of England's historic environment should be acknowledged as an extended database, created and curated by a network of contributing partners, which will include the RCHME, English Heritage and SMRs. Within this network, separate institutions would remain free to acquire the kinds of data they need for their own purposes, but with the benefit of being able to share and compare information across local, regional and national boundaries.

The foundations for a new partnership between local SMRs and the Royal Commission have already been laid, but must in future be strengthened and refined if England's historic monuments are to receive the documentation they need and deserve. It is to promote that co-operative effort that this report is now published. The encouragement and support of the Association of County Archaeological Officers, the Association of District Archaeological Officers, English Heritage and the many individual SMRs have greatly assisted us in the course of our survey.

TOM HASSALL, SECRETARY

Abbreviations

ACAO	Association of County Archaeological Officers
ADAO	Association of District Archaeological Officers
CBA	Council for British Archaeology
DNH	Department of National Heritage
DoE	Department of the Environment
EH	English Heritage
GDO	General Development Order
GIS	Geographic Information System
GLC	Greater London Council
GLSMR	Greater London Sites and Monuments Record
KPMG	Peat Marwick McLintock
MPP	Monuments Protection Programme
MVRG	Medieval Village Research Group
NAR	National Archaeological Record
NBR	National Buildings Record
NLAP	National Library of Air Photographs
NMR	National Monuments Record
OS	Ordnance Survey
PC	personal computer
PPG 16	Policy and Planning Guidance Note 16
RAF	Royal Air Force
RCAHMS	Royal Commission on the Ancient and Historical Monuments of Scotland
RCAHMW	Royal Commission on Ancient and Historical Monuments in Wales
RCHME	Royal Commission on the Historical Monuments of England
SMR	Sites and Monuments Record
SSA	Standard Spending Assessment

Summary of Conclusions

1 The Royal Commission on the Historical Monuments of England (RCHME) is England's national body of archaeological and architectural survey and record. Initially its detailed national inventory was compiled on a county by county basis, but from 1983 it has been responsible also for the comprehensive National Non-Intensive Record of archaeological sites previously compiled and held by the Ordnance Survey. These combined records now form part of the National Monuments Record (NMR).

GENERAL

2 In the 1970s and 1980s Sites and Monuments Records (SMRs) were established in all counties in England, their principal purpose being to supply local planning authorities with information on the location and importance of archaeological sites, but also to serve the needs of education and research. Almost all SMRs took as their starting point the Ordnance Survey Record, or, from 1983 onwards, the combined records now held by the RCHME.

3 From the 1980s both the RCHME and the SMRs began to hold their site records in computerised databases. An agreement to exchange data has led increasingly to the digital transfer of information. In four instances an SMR has now commenced or recommenced with a copy of the RCHME digital database.

4 From 1989 the RCHME has been responsible for the oversight of local Sites and Monuments Records. In a preliminary statement on how this partnership between SMRs and the NMR might be developed it was agreed with the Association of County Archaeological Officers (ACAO) that the combined contents of the National Archaeological Record and of the county SMRs be seen as the 'extended national archaeological database'. In exercising this responsibility the RCHME liaises with English Heritage, taking into account the latter's role as archaeological adviser with respect to the development control process and monument protection.

5 During 1993/4 the computerised databases held by the RCHME, including the National Archaeological Record (NAR), the National Library of Air Photographs (NLAP) and the National Buildings Record (NBR), will be transferred to a new unified NMR system. Within this system, the core data for a monument will be linked to a variety of more detailed records, which may include both archaeological and architectural surveys.

6 The unified NMR will continue to provide information required at a national or regional level. Particularly important will be data relating to the general state of the nation's archaeological and architectural heritage, such as the relative proportions of surviving and protected sites of different types and periods. The use of SMRs will also continue to increase, with the rapid implementation of PPG 16, and it is hoped this will encourage their use for other important non-planning matters.

FUTURE USE
AND COVERAGE

7 Current programmes are already directed to extending the coverage of both the NMR and SMRs in areas of current weakness; for instance so that all archaeological sites to 1945 are included. We recommend further record enhancement, to allow the quantification of sites destroyed, surviving and/or protected, and the validation of sites recorded but not yet checked in the field to required standards.

Costs

8 It is estimated that in 1991/2 the cost of maintaining the NMR was £1.69m. In the same year the expenditure on SMRs was c £3m. As the respective record systems increase in size there will be some increase in maintenance costs, and it is important that all possible steps are taken to minimise duplication of effort. The work of enhancement commenced through the *This Common Inheritance* initiative will need to be continued to ensure that SMRs are fully consistent with both national and local needs. We recommend that the Department of National Heritage (DNH) provides funding for this in advance of local government reorganisation.

The extended national archaeological record

9 The extended national archaeological database will itself widen the scope of the unified NMR. For each archaeological or architectural site represented in the unified NMR there will be a record containing essential core data: site number, NGR, address, site/building type, date, etc. Many of these records will have been created through data exchange with SMRs. Linked to this core data will be the more detailed information held or indexed only partly on computer, from RCHME investigative work, in SMRs and in English Heritage's Scheduled Monuments records.

10 We recommend that the RCHME, SMRs and English Heritage (EH) jointly examine the means of linking this information, where computerised, through data transfer or networking, thereby facilitating access for themselves and others to each organisation's data.

Updating the archaeological record

11 The RCHME and SMRs update their records through a process of primary recording, essentially updating or creating a core record for each site, together with essential descriptive and bibliographic data. We recommend that where this work can be undertaken from local sources, it be carried out in future by SMRs, on the basis that RCHME support and/or training will be available where necessary, and that the primary recording data be made available to the RCHME. In turn, the RCHME would be responsible for primary recording from national sources, with the data being similarly available to SMRs. We recommend that the data exchange agreement with the ACAO be revised to take account of these needs. We recommend that RCHME specialist staff continue to co-ordinate all maritime recording.

Historic buildings records

12 Several SMRs already hold records on historic buildings. In view of the forthcoming feasibility study instigated by the DNH on the national computerisation of the lists, which will be completed by the end of the financial year, we recommend that SMRs do not embark upon a programme of enhancement of these records.

Urban SMRs

13 In the 1990s a joint RCHME and EH initiative will create upwards of thirty urban databases, effectively SMRs for major historic towns hitherto poorly covered in existing county-based records. Databases for six towns have already been created. We recommend that these urban databases should wherever possible be linked to existing SMRs but at the same time utilise the new RCHME software package for SMRs, so as to avoid the proliferation of different record systems and to serve as a means by which the national record can be readily updated. Through data transfer or networking the urban databases could then have easy access to RCHME information particularly relevant to urban archaeology, including archaeological excavations and architectural data. In setting up new urban databases the RCHME and EH should ensure that the relationship between the new record and the existing SMR is clearly defined.

14 The recent review of the National Parks has recommended that for each there be available an archaeological database. We recommend that wherever possible this be achieved through links to the existing county SMR(s) or to the extended unified NMR, either by data transfer or by networking.

NATIONAL PARKS

15 The Association of District Archaeologists (ADAO) acknowledges that all district authorities should have access to an SMR. We recommend that wherever possible this be achieved through links to the existing county SMR or to the extended unified NMR, either by data transfer or by networking.

DISTRICT AUTHORITIES

16 We recommend that provision of a full range of SMR services and expertise may sometimes prove impracticable in areas significantly smaller than a traditional rural county or large historic town. Following the conclusions of the current review of local government reorganisation, we recommend that new local authorities should be statutorily required to establish their own staffed SMRs, networked to the extended unified NMR, or make provision jointly to support the original SMR and its archaeological staff.

LOCAL GOVERNMENT REORGANISATION

17 The SMR for Greater London (GLSMR) is held by EH. We recommend that EH and the RCHME discuss the relationship of the GLSMR with the NMR with a view to future networking of information. This would eliminate the extra costs arising from inputting much of the same archaeological and architectural data by the two national organisations.

GREATER LONDON SMR

18 Interest has already been expressed by EH in linking the computerised record of Scheduled Monuments in England to the archaeological information in the unified NMR. We recommend that the RCHME and EH proceed to network these records, partly to demonstrate the value of data networking for other areas where decisions still remain to be taken.

SCHEDULED MONUMENTS

19 We recommend that SMRs should not normally contain archival collections. Unique unpublished material should instead be deposited within an appropriate local museum, record office or the NMR.

RELATED ARCHIVES

20 An extended national archaeological database cannot function without agreement on areas relating to availability of data, notably copyright, ownership and charging. We recommend that a joint RCHME, ACAO, ADAO and EH working party be established to address these issues and recommend possible policies.

AVAILABILITY OF DATA

21 Although the NMR and most SMRs have followed broadly similar general principles of recording, there is a need for greater consistency between records. A smaller number of SMRs compiled with a hierarchical structure form a distinct group with which data transfer and networking will present some difficulty. We recommend that the work of the RCHME/ACAO Information Standards Working Party be extended to provide agreed standards for the structure of SMRs and for the cartographic information held as part of the SMR. RCHME support would be directed at subsequent necessary recasting or restructuring.

DATA STANDARDS

22 The RCHME is committed to supplying a computer package compatible with the unified NMR in 1993. Already seven SMRs are using an RCHME phase 1 package based on the computerised NAR. The new software should incorporate agreed data standards, and should facilitate future data transfer and networking.

COMPUTER SOFTWARE FOR SMRs

GEOGRAPHIC INFORMATION SYSTEMS

23 We recommend that the RCHME, ACAO and ADAO should monitor Geographic Information System (GIS) developments within local authorities, identifying common data standards for the transfer of information.

IMMEDIATE TASKS

24 Where RCHME action is required, proposals set out above will be incorporated in the next RCHME Corporate Plan.

1

INTRODUCTION

The Royal Commission on the Historical Monuments of England (RCHME) is England's national body of archaeological and architectural survey and record. From 1989 the RCHME has been responsible for the oversight of the local Sites and Monuments Records (SMRs) maintained by local authorities in each of England's forty-six shire counties and metropolitan areas.

SMRs have been established principally to enable county and district archaeologists to provide information and advice about archaeological sites to the local authority planning system. Their work is of direct relevance to the RCHME (charged with the development of a national database of the historic environment) and English Heritage (responsible for ensuring that nationally important elements of the historic environment are adequately protected and conserved).

The purpose of this Review is to assess the current effectiveness of local SMRs in England and to consider how they may be improved and strengthened to meet the changing needs of local authorities, the RCHME and English Heritage.

1.1 SCOPE AND PURPOSE OF THE SMR REVIEW

The RCHME was established in 1908 to 'make an inventory of the Ancient and Historical Monuments and Constructions connected with or illustrative of the contemporary culture, civilisation, and conditions of life of the people in England, excluding Monmouthshire, from the earliest times to the year 1700'. Similar Royal Commissions had been established in the previous year in Scotland and Wales. During the first sixty years of its life the Royal Commission for England pursued this task in two main ways: through field investigation and survey, and by acquiring and curating archives of photographs, drawings and documentary accounts relating to archaeological sites and historic buildings. In 1963 this work was much augmented by the incorporation within the Commission of the National Buildings Record. The results of each of these activities collectively constitute the National Monuments Record for England.

By the early 1980s the terminal date for the inclusion of monuments within the inventory had been extended progressively to c 1850 or later where appropriate. Fifteen counties had been covered wholly or partially by published inventories, while further areas had been covered by thematic studies. From the 1960s the latter included surveys directed at areas where monuments were threatened with destruction, through forestry, farming, quarrying, urban expansion and the construction of new towns.

The Ordnance Survey's involvement in the recording of archaeological sites has a long history (Phillips 1980). Major milestones were first the appointment of an archaeology officer in 1921 and then from 1947 onwards the construction of a National Non-Intensive Record of all antiquities (archaeological and historic sites, major historic buildings) in Great Britain. By 1983 this record, consisting of a card index with associated maps, contained c 130,000 records. The purpose of this record was to provide the authority for the depiction of antiquities on the nation's maps. In reviewing the functions and organisation of the Ordnance Survey the Serpell Committee recommended that this work would be more appropriately placed within the three RCHMs (Serpell 1979). The transfer of these functions in 1983 enabled the compilation of the comprehensive non-intensive record to be linked to the inventory work undertaken by the three RCHMs.

Since 1983 the part of the record for England held by the RCHME has been known as the National Archaeological Record (NAR), itself part of the National Monuments

1.2 THE DEVELOPMENT OF THE NATIONAL RECORD OF ARCHAEOLOGICAL SITES AND MONUMENTS

Record (NMR). The NAR has been augmented by continuing RCHME archival recording, ground and air survey, and, following agreement on data exchange with the Association of County Archaeological Officers (ACAO), one source of new information has been records known to SMRs but not yet included in the NAR. A second major enhancement of the record has been its computerisation, completed in 1988 and providing both text and map retrieval (Aberg and Leech 1992).

1·3 THE DEVELOPMENT OF LOCAL RECORDS OF ARCHAEOLOGICAL SITES AND MONUMENTS

By the 1960s there was a growing awareness of the rate at which archaeological sites were being damaged or destroyed and the corresponding need for the information amassed by the RCHMs and Ordnance Survey to be available to the local authority planning system. A critical step was the establishment in 1966 of a Committee of Enquiry into the Arrangements for the Protection of Field Monuments, the 'Walsh' Committee. In addition to recommending the strengthening of existing legislation for the protection of ancient monuments, the Walsh Committee concluded that the local authority planning system could in future serve a vital part in identifying and actively moderating threats to the historic environment:

> *A consolidated record of all known field monuments should be held by the County Planning Authorities so that they may be aware of all such monuments in their areas.*
>
> *County Councils which have not already done so should consider whether adequate professional archaeological assistance is available to them and should examine whether the appointment of an archaeological officer on a full or part-time basis is called for in their areas.* (Walsh 1969)

By 1969 one or two English counties had appointed archaeological officers and others had begun to compile experimental Sites and Monuments Records. From 1969 the Department of the Environment (DoE) encouraged the establishment of county archaeologists and SMRs (DoE 1972), so that by 1984 all but one English county possessed some form of SMR and access to the advice of a professional archaeologist (Burrow 1984, 10).

Since 1984 English Heritage (as the successor to the DoE Inspectorate of Ancient Monuments) has continued to promote the preservation of archaeological sites and landscapes through local authority strategic planning and tactical development control. Local authorities have been encouraged to assume responsibility for the maintenance of local SMRs and their core staff, through the provision of pump-priming grant aid. In the 1990s English Heritage has progressively reduced its financial support for the core functions of SMR database maintenance and information supply, but has continued, with the RCHME, to provide support for selected programmes of record enhancement and development control.

In addition to supporting the local planning and advisory role of SMRs, English Heritage has consistently acknowledged their importance as sources of information for its own national programmes. In 1984 an analysis of the number and diversity of sites recorded in SMRs demonstrated the inadequacy of the existing schedule of 12,500 legally protected ancient monuments (DoE 1984). This in turn led to the inauguration of the Monuments Protection Programme (MPP), an initiative designed to ensure legal protection for up to 50,000 to 60,000 nationally important monuments and sites. The MPP is scheduled for completion by the year 2007 and throughout its lifetime will have depended on local SMRs as its primary sources of information about the location, character and condition of sites to be considered for protection. The RCHME, through targeted air photographic mapping, is another main source.

Local authorities in England are under no statutory obligation to maintain SMRs; they do so only voluntarily on the basis of central government advice. The establishment of SMRs by local authorities was first formally recommended by government in 1972 (DoE 1972). The Town and Country Planning General

Development Order 1988 subsequently confirmed the legal status of SMRs by noting that a 'site of archaeological interest' means land which, *inter alia*, 'is within a site registered in any record kept by a county council and known as a County Sites and Monuments Record' (DoE 1988, 6). In 1990, the role of local SMRs was re-confirmed in the government's White Paper on the environment (DoE 1990*a*, 132, para 9.31) and further clarified by a Policy and Planning Guidance Note (PPG 16) confirming that SMRs should be recognised by planners and developers as the standard local sources of archaeological information and advice (DoE 1990*b*). In 1992, the RCHME's revised Royal Warrant, assigning to it 'responsibility for the oversight of local Sites and Monuments Records', provided further government recognition of the existence of SMRs.

1.4 THE NEED FOR A REVIEW OF SMRs

The convergence of interest between the RCHME and SMRs was formally acknowledged by the Policy Review carried out in 1988 by the sponsor departments of the three separate Royal Commissions for England, Scotland and Wales. Recognising the need for a clearly defined relationship between national and local records, it was recommended that:

> *The Royal Commissions make it a priority to establish, in consultation with local producers and keepers of data, a strategy for databases at national and local level ... in order to establish what needs to be held at the national level, and where the national database simply needs to provide an index to more detailed sources of information held locally.* (KPMG 1988, 93)

More explicitly, a Royal Commission responsibility for local SMRs was recognised (KPMG 1988, 98) to be the most effective means of:

- ❖ avoiding duplication of effort;
- ❖ setting and monitoring standards of recording;
- ❖ ensuring co-operation rather than rivalry between the NMR and SMRs.

Responding to the KPMG report, the Department of the Environment announced that the RCHME would henceforth be 'recognised as the lead national body for oversight of the system of local Sites and Monuments Records in England', but declined to implement a further recommendation that a 'sum equivalent to the average total per annum grant to local SMRs from English Heritage be transferred to the Royal Commission' (KPMG 1988, 98). It was also confirmed that in exercising its responsibility the RCHME 'must liaise with English Heritage, and take account of their interest in SMRs as an input to the Monuments Protection Programme and to local decision-making and conservation generally'.

A first definition of this new 'lead role' for SMRs was provided by the RCHME in 1990 following agreement with the Association of County Archaeological Officers:

> *The Royal Commission views its relationship to county SMRs essentially as a partnership and its role very much as a co-operative and co-ordinating one. Our common concern is with:*
>
> - ❖ *the acquisition, vetting, ordering and storage of archaeological information (used in its widest sense and thus including extant buildings), as required at national and local level;*
> - ❖ *its use for a range of purposes (eg, planning, conservation, management, tourism, education, research) also at both national and local level;*
> - ❖ *and its ready accessibility to members of the public.*
>
> *SMRs maintain for planning purposes a register of archaeological sites and monuments in their respective counties. At a local level their work parallels and extends the national role of the RCHME. The Royal Commission regards the combined contents of the National Archaeological Record and of the*

county SMRs as the extended national archaeological database and recognises the pressing need to complete and enhance that database.

(RCHME 1990a, 23)

Following further discussions with the Association of County Archaeological Officers, this review of SMRs was commenced in December 1991.

1.5 OBJECTIVES OF THE SMR REVIEW

The principal objectives of the RCHME review of SMRs in England have been to:

- review the current functions and organisation of the NAR/NMR and SMRs (Chapters 2 and 3);
- identify and compare the scope and content of the NAR/NMR and SMRs (Chapter 4);
- make recommendations on the future functions and organisation of the NAR/NMR and SMRs, with special reference to the future responsibilities of the RCHME and the possible reorganisation of local government in England (Chapters 5 and 6);
- review the needs for harmonisation of standards of SMR, NMR and EH documentation, computerisation and data exchange (Chapter 6).

1.6 METHODOLOGY

The RCHME study was carried out in three main stages:

- a review of existing literature, including previous studies of the SMR system by English Heritage, the Association of County Archaeological Officers and others; statutory and advisory documents issued by government, the Council of Europe, English Heritage and other official bodies; the RCHME Policy Review (1988), Royal Warrant (1992) and other documentation prepared by or on behalf of the RCHME;
- circulation of a questionnaire seeking factual information on the current organisation, funding and content of SMRs and opinion on their future priorities and requirements in the fields of record enhancement, information supply, computerisation and training;
- the carrying out of confidential face-to-face interviews to explore further the priorities, problems and perceived needs of county archaeologists and other staff responsible for the management of the SMRs contributing to the survey.

In the course of the survey, factual information and opinion was received from each of England's forty-six county and metropolitan SMRs; from two National Parks currently in the process of establishing SMR databases, and from the National Trust.

At the outset of the survey the Royal Commission was aware of the existence of a number of additional local SMRs serving the specialised needs of some rural and urban areas in England. In view of their small number and very varied constitutional positions it was not appropriate to include them within the initial round of data collection, although their role and position is recognised and discussed elsewhere in this report.

In addition to seeking the views of individual SMRs and county archaeologists our survey has benefited from further interviews and discussions with the Associations of County and District Archaeological Officers, English Heritage and other relevant parties.

Factual information provided by individual SMRs is held on file by the RCHME and will not be disclosed without the written authority of the supplier. It is intended that this information should in future be regularly updated to allow the RCHME to monitor effectively the development and needs of the local SMR system in line with its lead role responsibility. General information on SMRs, much obtained through this Review, will be available in the future to users of the RCHME information systems.

2

THE ROYAL COMMISSION ON THE HISTORICAL MONUMENTS OF ENGLAND AND THE NATIONAL MONUMENTS RECORD

2·1 THE ROYAL COMMISSION ON THE HISTORICAL MONUMENTS OF ENGLAND

The functions of the Royal Commission on the Historical Monuments of England (RCHME) are set out in its Royal Warrant, reissued in April 1992. In brief, the RCHME's task is to compile and assess, curate and make available the national record of England's ancient monuments and historic buildings for the use of individuals and bodies concerned with understanding, interpreting and managing the historic environment.

The RCHME fulfils its functions through:

❖ maintaining and curating the National Monuments Record (NMR) as the national record of the historic environment;

❖ identifying, surveying and recording buildings, sites and ancient monuments of archaeological, architectural and historical interest in England and its territorial waters, in order both to enhance and update the NMR and to respond to public interest and statutory needs;

❖ recording listed buildings before demolition or significant alteration;

❖ continuing and furthering the work of the Survey of London;

❖ promoting the use of information available in the NMR by all appropriate means, including publication;

❖ exercising national responsibility for the oversight of local Sites and Monuments Records;

❖ collecting and exchanging data with other record holders and providing an index to data from other sources;

❖ establishing and maintaining national standards in investigation and interpretation, and in the curating of records relating to archaeology and historic architecture, and providing guidance to other bodies;

❖ providing advice and information relevant to the preservation and conservation of buildings, sites and ancient monuments of archaeological, architectural and historic interest.

2·2 THE NATIONAL MONUMENTS RECORD

The National Monuments Record is central to the functions of the RCHME. It is a permanent, publicly accessible source of information, and is in three main parts: the National Archaeological Record (NAR), the National Buildings Record (NBR) and the National Library of Air Photographs (NLAP). These three sections are together responsible for:

❖ creating a national database of information about sites and buildings of historic and architectural interest;

❖ curating national collections of associated photographs, drawings and documents;

❖ providing a service of information and advice to government and the general public.

Following the issuing of its revised Royal Warrant (1992) the RCHME has embarked on a systematic review of the future functions and priorities of the NMR. The initial conclusions of that review process are discussed in greater detail in Chapter 6 of this report. For the present, a summary account is provided of the main current functions of each of the three sections of the NMR.

2.3 THE NATIONAL ARCHAEOLOGICAL RECORD – CORE FUNCTIONS AND PRIORITIES

The core functions and priorities of the NAR may be summarised as:

- maintenance of a core text and map-based record of all terrestrial and offshore maritime sites of archaeological significance dating from the earliest times to 1945;
- curation of an archive of plans, photographs and descriptive accounts prepared in the course of RCHME programmes of archaeological survey;
- creating a national index of archaeological archives and the copying, cataloguing and curating of those deemed to be of national importance;
- maintenance of a national index of archaeological excavations and other archaeological fieldwork;
- retrieval and supply of data to government agencies, SMRs and the general public, including archaeological information for inclusion on Ordnance Survey maps;
- encouragement of common national standards of archaeological recording and documentation;
- identification of national priorities for further investigative survey and record enhancement.

2.4 THE NATIONAL BUILDINGS RECORD

The NBR is a separate section of the NMR and differs from the NAR in several important respects. These arise in part from its independent historical development as an archive of photographs and plans rather than as a formally structured database of sites. More importantly, they reflect the specialised requirements of architectural historians and the different statutory and organisational framework within which the country's stock of historic buildings is managed and protected.

Like the NAR, the NBR is currently carrying out a systematic review of its functions, priorities and working methods. In the past, the interface between the NBR and SMRs has been much more limited than has been the case with the NAR. Instead, the NBR's principal connections have tended to be with English Heritage, district level planning and conservation officers and other individuals and institutions concerned with the study and care of standing buildings. The RCHME is nevertheless aware of the increasing interest now being shown by county and urban SMRs in the maintenance of local records of historic buildings. If a current RCHME proposal to computerise the Statutory Lists of Historic Buildings is implemented, there is likely to be a greater demand from local authorities and others to access architectural information from the NBR via, or in association with, the computer-based list.

At present the core activities and priorities of the NBR may be summarised as:

- curating and enhancing a national archive of some three million photographs, plans, drawings and descriptive accounts of English architecture, including those prepared in the course of the RCHME's own programmes of investigative recording;
- systematic cataloguing and computerised indexing of the NBR collections;
- encouraging the development of a core computerised text record of all listed and unlisted buildings of architectural and historic importance;

- maintaining the national publicly accessible collection of Statutory Lists of Historic Buildings;
- provision of a public search room and information service on behalf of official and public users of the NBR;
- identification of priorities for further investigative survey and photographic recording;
- compilation of national inventories of specific classes of architectural structure or fitment (eg, war memorials; medieval stained glass).

2·5 THE NATIONAL LIBRARY OF AIR PHOTOGRAPHS

In addition to its archaeological and architectural divisions, the NMR maintains a national collection of air photographs whose subject matter straddles and transcends the thematic interests of the NBR and NAR. Based on a core collection of half a million aerial photographs of archaeological sites, the NLAP has been expanded by the progressive transfer to the NMR of 3·5 million RAF, Ordnance Survey and commercial air photographs dating from the 1940s to the present day.

In addition to its value as a record of the existence, character and changing condition of historic monuments, the NLAP collection is a unique source of information about other aspects of the natural and man-made environment. Accordingly, the RCHME has given high priority to the cataloguing of the collection and to the development of a computerised information retrieval system on behalf of official and public users. The resulting 'Photonet' system now provides access to more than 1·5 million separate photographs. At present it exists in isolation from the NMR's archaeological and architectural databases, but is due to be linked directly to these by the end of 1994.

The main aims and activities of the NLAP may be summarised as:

- acquisition of aerial photographs taken in the course of current RCHME-funded programmes of aerial survey and collections of older aerial photographs deemed to be of national importance;
- curating and computerised cataloguing of the NLAP's collections of oblique and vertical photographs;
- provision of a public service of information retrieval, library consultation and photographic copying;
- encouragement of harmonised national standards of air photographic conservation and documentation;
- support for air photographic collections housed within local SMRs.

At present the NLAP shares two main areas of interest with local SMRs. The first of these involves the use of the NLAP collections for identifying and mapping sites and areas of archaeological interest. The second concerns the long-standing co-operation between the RCHME and SMRs with regard to the printing and cataloguing of archaeological air photographs. The RCHME assumed responsibility for the co-ordination of archaeological air photography in England in 1985. Since then a variety of initiatives has helped to create more effective and economical operational relationships between the NLAP and individual SMRs that hold collections of aerial photographs. In addition to syndicated approaches to the processing and printing of negatives, these include the adoption of core data standards for the cataloguing of aerial photographs and the routine exchange of information about newly indexed material.

2·6 COMPUTERISATION OF THE NMR

The RCHME began to exploit computers for the storage and retrieval of information in the early 1980s. The largest of these projects was the computerisation of the NAR (Hart and Leech 1989; Aberg and Leech 1992). By the end of the decade it had developed a number of separate databases running on a range of host computers (Table 1). Following the development of the NAR and NLAP systems, the decision was taken in 1987 that Oracle should be the standard database system in use throughout the RCHME.

TABLE 1 PRINCIPAL RCHME DATABASES MAINTAINED AT 31 MARCH 1992

Name of database	Host computer	Database and operating system
NAR Monuments/Archaeological Sites	VAX 11/750	Oracle/VMS
NAR Excavation Index	Compaq	Informix/Unix
NAR Photographic Index	Compaq	Informix/Unix
NAR Microfilm Archive Index	Compaq	Informix/Unix
Archaeological Thesaurus	VAX 11/750	Oracle/VMS
NAR Library Catalogue	VAX 11/750	Oracle/VMS
NBR Buildings Index	Compaq	Informix/Unix
NBR Stained Glass Index	Compaq	Informix/Unix
Architectural Thesaurus	Compaq	Informix/Unix
Threatened Buildings	Compaq	Informix/Unix
NLAP Photonet Index	Microvax2	GIMMS/Oracle/VMS

GEOGRAPHIC INFORMATION SYSTEMS

At present the NAR and NLAP each possess facilities that allow geographical searching of their indexes and the automated production of distribution maps. In addition, the RCHME's archaeological and architectural surveyors use a range of computer-aided systems for the production of measured plans and drawings. A consultancy to identify a central RCHME strategy in developing its policy to GIS began in December 1992.

IMAGE RETRIEVAL SYSTEMS

The NMR is actively examining the longer term potential of optical disk and related digital systems for the storage and retrieval of its photographic collections. A pilot project has been developed utilising records from the RCHME's investigations and surveys in York.

THE UNIFIED NMR

In 1990 the RCHME commissioned an analysis of its own use of computerised information and of its operational requirements for the future. This initial study resulted in the definition of an RCHME Information Systems Strategy (Oracle 1990) which recommended the construction of a new unified NMR database linking the existing NAR, NBR and NLAP databases and associated functions. By 1994 this system will support the input and retrieval of information by staff throughout the RCHME's network of national and local offices.

Within this single NMR the core data for each site will be shared by a variety of more detailed records. Users of the NMR will not only have direct access to the whole of the core national record of buildings and archaeological sites, but will be able to identify simultaneously any associated drawings, written accounts, ground photographs and aerial photographs housed in the NMR archive. The unified NMR will therefore provide a comprehensive computerised record relating monuments to events/activities and archives. This will allow close monitoring of England's national heritage through the quantification and monitoring of monuments and buildings and the recording activities carried out on them.

2·7
PUBLIC ACCESS TO INFORMATION IN THE NMR

The NMR is constituted as a publicly accessible record. Its collections of photographs, drawings, published works and unpublished written records are thus openly available to all categories of official and private user. The only exception to this rule is when access has to be restricted by the terms of Official Secrets and Data Protection Acts, or in order to protect buildings and archaeological sites from illegal damage and theft.

The majority of the NMR's extensive photographic holdings have traditionally been available on unrestricted access in the public search rooms of the NBR, NAR and NLAP. More recently, the increasing size of the collections and concerns for the safety of unique material has in some areas required a withdrawal from the principle of direct and unsupervised access.

Access to information held within the NMR's computerised databases is similarly free of restriction, exceptions normally being made only in the case of fields containing supporting personal or confidential management information. In recent years the Royal Commission has nevertheless recognised the risk that may be posed to certain categories of monument through the unrestricted supply of computer-held information.

In this context the Royal Commission is concerned not only with the views of English Heritage, SMRs and other UK bodies, but also with recent Council of Europe initiatives for the protection of the cultural heritage. In particular, the British government's signing of the Revised European Convention on the Protection of the Archaeological Heritage (1992) is expected to place pressure on the NMR to comply with European standards governing the free exchange of cultural heritage information.

2·8
USE OF THE NMR

In addition to allowing public consultation of its collections, the NMR supplies information on request from its catalogues and databases and provides photographic copies of material held in its archives.

In 1991/2 the NMR as a whole responded to 15,243 government or public enquiries. The pattern of usage nevertheless varies between different sections of record. In the case of the NBR, the majority of enquiries continue to come from researchers, amenity societies, publishers, English Heritage and the general public. By contrast, the NAR and the NLAP receive much larger numbers of requests from SMRs, archaeological units and archaeological, environmental and land use consultants.

In 1990 a study of NMR services and usage was carried out on behalf of the Royal Commission (Coopers & Lybrand Deloitte 1990). A key concern of the review was to examine ways in which the NMR could improve the range and quality of its services. Following the recommendation of this study, the Royal Commission has appointed a Marketing Manager to oversee the development of NMR marketing and to ensure that information is supplied in ways which best suit the needs of external users.

Amongst initiatives currently under consideration are the development of optical disk and on-line computerised enquiry systems that would allow access to NMR information from remote locations. In addition, the transfer of the Royal Commission's headquarters to Swindon in 1994 will allow much easier access to NMR collections currently dispersed between offices and stores in central London, outer London and Southampton.

2·9
USE OF DATA IN THE NMR FOR RCHME PUBLICATIONS

The Royal Commission publishes the results of its survey and recording work in a variety of formats. Traditionally this was achieved through the publication of county inventories. Since the mid 1980s, the Royal Commission has adopted a more flexible publication policy that allows the dissemination of information at a variety of levels.

The cornerstone of this policy is the principle that exhaustive publication of information is no longer feasible or desirable. The central aim should instead be to provide a guide and overview to information permanently archived and accessible within the NMR. This is currently achieved through:

❖ conventionally published monographs and contributions to academic journals;
❖ desk-top published specialist reports and papers for more limited circulation;
❖ structured user guides to NMR collections and services.

Enhancement of the current range of NMR user guides in line with the development of the unified NMR and on-line systems of research and information retrieval has been identified as a key priority for the future. In addition, the Royal Commission recognises the medium and long-term potential of electronic media for the dissemination of textual and graphical information and proposes to explore further the application of imaging technology during 1993/4.

2.10 Copyright and charging for information in the NMR

Written records, photographs and drawings created by staff of the Royal Commission are all subject to Crown Copyright, as are information and archival items acquired from other government departments and agencies. Crown Copyright is inalienable and amongst other NMR material covers Ordnance Survey Archaeology Division record cards, DoE 'Greenback' Listed Building descriptions and RAF air photographs.

In addition, the NMR holds large numbers of photographs and written reports that remain the copyright of private individuals, local authorities and commercial organisations. It is the policy of the Royal Commission to protect any such interests that can be clearly defined. It is nevertheless recognised that true ownership can often no longer be proved. Sometimes it has also for practical purposes to be accepted (as in the case of jointly sponsored work) as shared between numbers of individuals and institutions.

Under the terms of the Copyright, Designs and Patents Act (1988), contractors or recipients of grants normally retain copyright title to any work they carry out on behalf of a client or sponsor. However, to meet the requirements of Her Majesty's Stationery Office, the Royal Commission will in future be under pressure to ensure that copyright in any such commissioned work is assigned to the Crown.

In line with the practices of the British Library, Public Record Office and comparable institutions, access to NMR information and archival material has traditionally been provided free of charge to both official and private users. However, for many years charges have been made for the publication of Crown Copyright material and the supply of photographic prints, photocopies and computer listings.

In advance of the publication of a full charging and pricing policy, it seems likely that basic access to the NMR's core collections will remain free of charge. However, fees will be levied increasingly for manual searches, on-line information services, expert advice and other value-added products. A fee-paying express information service has already been introduced to meet the needs of commercial and professional users of the NLAP and similar initiatives are expected to be launched within other divisions of the NMR during 1993.

Certain categories of user may in future be exempted from some or all charges on the grounds of standing agreements for the exchange of information and data. Relationships of this kind already exist between the Royal Commission and English Heritage, the Ordnance Survey and other bodies funded through government, but may in future need to be extended to include SMRs and academic institutions.

2·11 LIAISON WITH SMRs

Formal channels of communication between the NMR and SMRs are provided through standing RCHME/ACAO and RCHME/ADAO liaison committees. Several of those interviewed in this Review expressed concern about the effectiveness of these current channels of communication. At one level it was argued that the frequent necessity to negotiate with separate branches of the NMR appeared to outside eyes complicated and confusing.

At a second level it was suggested that the lack of common points of contact made it difficult for SMRs to gain a clear appreciation of the RCHME's overall objectives and priorities. In particular, many county and district SMRs remain uncertain about:

- what the RCHME means in its references to an 'extended national record' and the 'networking' of information about the historic environment between local SMRs and the NMR;
- the roles that the RCHME envisages that SMRs and the NMR will respectively play in the creation and curation of the extended national record;
- the part that the NMR will play in the supply of information and advice about the historic environment, and the extent to which it will respect the legitimate interests and responsibilities of local SMRs in this sphere;
- the level of financial, technical and advisory support that the RCHME proposes to make available to local SMRs for the maintenance and enhancement of their records of the historic environment.

RCHME representatives attend the meetings of regional SMR Working Parties; these do not, however, cover the whole of England and some have become inactive. At an operational level, contact with SMRs is normally through the professional staff of the NAR, NBR and NLAP or via the Royal Commission's network of regionally based survey teams.

2·12 INFORMATION STANDARDS WORK

A major area of liaison to date has been the work on data standards undertaken by a joint Information Standards Working Party convened by the RCHME and the ACAO, and including representatives of EH and the British Archaeological Bibliography. This is in the process of agreeing a new framework of core data standards for the recording of archaeological information. These will include vocabulary control based on the RCHME/EH Archaeological Thesaurus and new national standards and protocols for the recording of archaeological bibliographic information agreed with the British Archaeological Bibliography. This work is being utilised both in the new data standards being produced jointly by the RCHME and EH for use in the urban databases being created in upwards of thirty historic towns, and in the national standards recently agreed for the recording of sites and wrecks in English territorial waters.

Further harmonisation of data standards will be achieved through the consolidation of existing thesauri of archaeological and architectural terms (RCHME and English Heritage 1989, 1992) into a single unified thesaurus for use by the NMR, English Heritage and other recording bodies. The recommendations of an RCHME/EH/ACAO working party are due for release in 1993.

In addition to assisting the development and co-ordination of standards of architectural and archaeological recording for England, the RCHME collaborates with associated organisations in other parts of the United Kingdom. It is also actively involved under the aegis of the Council of Europe in the formulation of common standards for the documentation of the cultural heritage within Europe. Information standards for the recording of sites and wrecks in English territorial waters have also drawn upon work in the United States and Canada.

Since 1986 a standing conference under the joint aegis of the RCHME and the Institute of Field Archaeologists has monitored the application of computer technology and standards throughout the archaeological profession.

2·13 Costs

The RCHME as a whole is funded through grant-in-aid from the Department of National Heritage, augmented by income from the sale of goods and services. In 1991/2, the RCHME employed 178·5 professional and support staff at an overall operating cost of £6·01m (Table 2). In turn, the three sections of the NMR employed sixty-four permanent and temporary staff at an aggregate cost of £1·6m, which included grant aid and contracts to SMRs and other outside bodies (Table 3).

TABLE 2 RCHME FUNCTIONAL EXPENDITURE 1991/2

	£k
SURVEY AND RECORDING	
Archaeology	1,161
Architecture	1,319
Subtotal	2,480
NATIONAL MONUMENTS RECORD	
NAR	898
NBR	534
NLAP	187
Subtotal	1,619
CENTRAL SERVICES	
Administration and marketing	503
Computer services	575
Photography	678
Publications	228
Subtotal	1,984
Total operational expenditure	6,083
Accommodation and relocation	2,160
Total RCHME expenditure	8,243

(Source: *Annual Report 1991/2*)

TABLE 3 NMR STAFFING AND OPERATING COSTS 1991/2

	Curating and recording		Information supply		Total	
	Staff	Cost (£k)	Staff	Cost (£k)	Staff	Cost (£k)
NAR	29	744	6	154	35	898
NBR	17	454	3	80	20	534
NLAP	5	104	4	83	9	187
Total	51	1,302	13	317	64	1,619

(Sources: *Annual Report 1991/2* and Corporate Plan)

3

LOCAL SITES AND MONUMENTS RECORDS IN ENGLAND

3.1 INTRODUCTION

Analysis of the current organisation, staffing and funding of SMRs in England is based on information provided to us by the county councils and the organisations now responsible for archaeological advice in the former metropolitan counties and Greater London, together providing SMR coverage for most of England. Information has also been obtained from two National Park authorities, the National Trust and a number of District Councils corresponding to major historic towns and a small number of other archaeological bodies, all responsible for smaller SMRs.

3.2 LOCAL SITES AND MONUMENTS RECORDS IN ENGLAND – CORE FUNCTIONS

The key task of county and district archaeologists is to provide professional archaeological advice to local planning authorities and others, and to monitor the implications of development plan policies and planning decisions.

The central purpose of SMRs held in local authorities is to maintain a database of archaeological and historic sites as an aid to their management and protection through the planning process. Beyond that primary objective the majority of SMRs share a range of additional core functions that include the supply of information and specialist advice to local planners and the further enhancement of the SMR record through documentary and field research. Thereafter, SMRs exhibit greater variation in the range and scope of their activities, depending upon the policies of their parent bodies and the individual strengths and interests of past and current county archaeologists and SMR officers. In particular, there are variations in:

❖ spheres of archaeological and architectural interest;
❖ sources of information and methods of recording;
❖ size and quality of the resulting SMR databases;
❖ supporting records and archives;
❖ progress with computerisation.

3.3 COUNTY AND METROPOLITAN SMRs

The largest number of SMRs are those serving England's forty-six shire and metropolitan counties. The oldest, the Oxfordshire SMR, was founded in the mid 1960s (Benson 1974) and by 1984 all but one county was in possession of some form of local record and the services of a professional archaeological adviser (Burrow 1984). A full national network was finally completed with the creation of a unified SMR for Kent in 1989. Throughout the later 1970s and early 1980s it was the policy of the Inspectorate of Ancient Monuments and (latterly) English Heritage to encourage county councils to take responsibility for the management of this system of local heritage records.

In the spirit of the recommendations of the Walsh Committee (Walsh 1969), county planning departments are the commonest home of county SMRs (23, or 48 per cent). The next largest concentration (12, or 24 per cent) of SMRs is within departments responsible for museum, library and leisure services, while seven others (15 per cent) are dispersed amongst sections responsible for property (Cambridgeshire, Humberside) and the environment (Northumberland,

Somerset), or are maintained as jointly funded service units (West Midlands, West Yorkshire, Cornwall).

Outside the conventional local authority structure SMRs for Greater Manchester, South Yorkshire and Lancashire are maintained on behalf of county, district and borough authorities by the Greater Manchester Archaeological Unit, Sheffield City Museum and the Lancaster University Archaeological Unit. A further exception is the SMR for Greater London, a collective record for the capital managed directly by English Heritage and discussed in greater detail elsewhere in this report.

The majority of county SMRs are organised so that the SMR is maintained and serviced by one or more SMR officers reporting to the county archaeologist. We touch elsewhere on the varying range of functions performed by county archaeologists and their departments. For the present it is relevant to note that county SMRs, whether maintained within planning departments or elsewhere, may be divided into three distinct categories:

- SMRs whose function is confined to the collection, interpretation and impartial dissemination of archaeological information to internal and external users;
- SMRs that are simultaneously responsible for the public supply of archaeological *information* and the provision of specialist archaeological *advice* to the local authority planning departments of which they are part;
- SMRs that are maintained as component parts of archaeological units responsible not only for providing archaeological information and planning-related advice, but for the practical execution of developer-funded archaeological survey and excavation.

3.4 Staffing levels of county and metropolitan SMRs

With the exception of Greater London, every county in England is now served by a county archaeologist whose salary is paid either wholly or in large part by local government (in Greater London, English Heritage provides an archaeological and advisory service analogous to those provided by local authorities elsewhere). In addition, the majority of SMRs are supported by at least one full-time SMR officer to ensure the safekeeping of the record and the supply of information and professional advice to internal and external users. A core element of the job of all SMR officers, and the one that consumes the largest proportion of their time, is to check and provide expert professional comment upon the archaeological implications of planning applications submitted to district planning offices and minerals applications lodged at county level. SMR officers are also responsible for the progressive enhancement and routine updating of the SMR database, although the majority of such work is in practice delegated to SMR assistants appointed on short-term contracts.

During 1991 England's forty-six counties and metropolitan areas were served by a total of 104 permanent staff compared with sixty-nine in 1986. This figure is made up of forty-five county archaeological advisers, plus fifty-nine SMR officers and assistants responsible both for development control work and for SMR maintenance and enhancement. This 50 per cent increase in the number of professional staff able to provide continuity of experience is warmly welcomed by both the RCHME and EH. Each supports the view of the ACAO and individual county archaeologists that the primary data contained in the SMR can only be effectively retrieved and interpreted by staff intimately familiar with the archaeology of the local region.

In addition to their permanent officers, county SMRs typically employ further staff on temporary contracts to assist with the updating, enhancement and computerisation of the SMR database. In 1991, the equivalent of seventy-one full-time posts were supported in England's forty-six county SMRs compared with forty-four posts in 1986. More than three-quarters (77 per cent) of the cost of these temporary posts was met, however, from outside sources. As a result, county archaeologists continue to complain of the difficulty of ensuring adequate continuity of expertise amongst staff responsible for the key job of building up a reliable and authoritative record of the local historic environment.

Because their short-term contracts depend on an intermittent and unpredictable flow of project funding from EH, the RCHME and other outside sources, younger and less experienced personnel responsible for SMR enhancement have only limited job security. The turnover of staff thus tends to be rapid and has consistently prevented investment in programmes of professional training designed to build up expertise in such areas as documentary research, bibliographic recording, field survey and air photo interpretation.

When county SMRs were first being compiled, and during a secondary phase of computerisation during the 1980s, there was little alternative to the employment of teams of temporary SMR staff on short-term contracts, large numbers of them supported through Manpower Services Commission job-creation schemes. It was nevertheless recognised that this approach was liable to be at the expense of reliability and consistency. At that early stage, the priority was necessarily to ensure breadth of coverage in advance of later improvement in the depth and accuracy of information about the historic landscape.

To meet the new needs of PPG 16, the key jobs of SMR assistants will, over the next ten years, be the systematic revision, enhancement and validation of those initial records to a new and uniform standard. In the view of the RCHME and the ACAO that goal will only be achieved if SMRs are able to employ recording staff in ways that allow the necessary development and retention of skills and local knowledge.

3.5 DISTRICT SMRs

Within the last few years an increasing number of England's 440 district, borough and city authorities have appointed their own archaeological advisers and community archaeologists. Of the twenty-four English members of the recently formed Association of District Archaeological Officers, twenty-two represent urban authorities and are based either in local planning departments or in museums or archaeological units; exceptions to the rule are ADAO members representing the rural districts of South Kesteven in Lincolnshire and the Test Valley in Hampshire.

In the 1990s a joint RCHME and EH initiative will create upwards of thirty urban databases, effectively SMRs for major historic towns poorly covered in existing county SMRs. Databases for Chester, Cirencester, Durham and York have already been created.

Apart from these historic towns, only a relatively small number of the bodies affiliated to the ADAO are known to have created formal SMRs of their own. These district level records have usually been established as a result of local initiative and their recording standards and criteria do not always conform with the record structure adopted by the corresponding county SMR. An additional cause of concern has been the lack of formal agreements for data exchange between some district-level records and county SMRs. In such cases there remains the potential for unacceptable duplication of effort both in the compilation of records and in the subsequent retrieval of information from overlapping but separately structured record systems.

3.6 NATIONAL PARK SMRs

Within the last five years five of England's seven National Parks have appointed their own archaeology officers to advise on the management and conservation of archaeological sites within the areas for which they have special planning responsibilities. At the outset National Park archaeology officers relied for their information on SMRs maintained by the one or more counties within which their Parks lay. More recently the Yorkshire Dales and North York Moors National Parks have each begun to compile specialised records of their own but in close co-operation with the NMR and existing North Yorkshire County Council SMR, with whom they have established informal agreements regarding data standards and the exchange of information. The North York Moors National Park has an on-line link to the North Yorkshire county SMR for interrogation purposes only.

It is possible that in future some National Parks will be accorded the status of unitary planning authorities, responsible for all aspects of development control and strategic land-use planning currently managed by district and county authorities. In anticipation of this increase in responsibility the Edwards Committee review of the National Park system has recently concluded that 'a comprehensive and comparative archaeological database for each National Park should be developed jointly by the various recording agencies' (Countryside Commission 1991). In response to this recommendation, the RCHME and the National Parks are currently examining the way in which such databases may be most effectively established and thereafter maintained as constituent parts of the extended national record of archaeological sites. Informal discussion suggests that many hope to retain access to county SMRs rather than develop independent systems.

3.7 THE NATIONAL TRUST

As England's third largest landowner, the National Trust is responsible for the conservation and management of an estimated 40,000 archaeological sites and 20,000 vernacular buildings, many of them grouped within historic landscapes of international importance. Because these sites are dispersed across the length and breadth of the country, the National Trust has developed a specialised archaeological database of its own. In addition to including conventional data about the location and character of each monument, the SMR is designed to provide National Trust land agents with deeper levels of information about the changing condition and management requirements of sites in their care.

In 1991 the National Trust employed a team of 9·5 permanent and four temporary archaeological surveyors and advisers. Although the SMR is maintained specifically as an internal management tool, the National Trust allows access to bona fide external enquirers and is currently discussing with the RCHME arrangements for the routine exchange of information with the NMR.

3.8 THE GREATER LONDON SMR

The development of an SMR system for Greater London has a complex history that reflects the differing needs and organisation of England's capital city. In 1983/4 the Greater London Council (GLC) resolved to establish an SMR for Greater London, in partnership with the Museum of London, Passmore Edwards Museum and Kingston Heritage Centre. Its aim was to provide a comprehensive coverage of the capital's known archaeological sites and 30,000 listed buildings. From the outset it was intended that the record would be held and maintained by the GLC's Historic Buildings Division, but the work of compiling the record was carried out under contract through the participating museums. Following the abolition of the GLC it was recognised that effective management of London's past would require the continued existence of a unified SMR that transcended local borough boundaries. Responsibility for the GLSMR was accordingly passed in 1986 to English Heritage, who continued the existing arrangements for compilation of the record. The compilation phase ended, as planned, in March 1992, since when English Heritage has had full responsibility for maintaining and updating the GLSMR, and for enhancing it as appropriate.

3.9 COMPUTERISATION OF SMRs

Early on in the development of county-level archaeological record systems, SMRs and the Inspectorate of Ancient Monuments recognised the critical importance of computerisation for effective retrieval and analysis of information about the historic environment. Following a series of pioneering computerisation projects in the late 1970s, thirty-one British SMRs were reported to possess some form of machine-retrievable record by 1984 (Burrow 1984, 11).

During this initial phase of development individual SMRs adopted a wide variety of hardware and software platforms for their databases. While some chose to base themselves on the mainframe computer systems supported by their parent local authorities, others opted for one or other of the many types of microcomputer that were then coming on to the market.

By the mid 1980s it had become apparent that this unco-ordinated development was seriously threatening the compatibility of data and the long-term potential for the exchange of information between SMRs and with other institutions. In response to this problem, in 1986 English Heritage issued an SMR database system known as 'Superfile' to replace a previous suite of microcomputer programs known colloquially as 'DoE Version 1'.

By 1988, the Superfile software package was being used by twenty-five county SMRs in England but was recognised to be reaching the end of its useful life. Accordingly, the RCHME agreed as part of its 'lead role' for SMRs to develop a replacement for the Superfile system. As an intermediate measure a simplified version of the existing NAR Oracle database system has been offered to SMRs with an urgent need to replace their current systems. Seven SMRs have thus far transferred to the interim SMR-Online system in advance of the design and building of a completely new software package in 1993.

Within the last few years the application of computerised information systems in SMRs has been the subject of a sequence of reviews (eg, Chadburn 1989; Lang 1990; Clubb 1990) and extensive professional discussion and debate. That debate is still in progress and it has not been the purpose of this present survey to carry out a detailed analysis of the current and future functional requirements of SMRs. Instead we have confined ourselves to:

❖ establishing a central register of software and hardware currently in use within local SMRs;

❖ recording the comments of county archaeologists concerning the effectiveness and limitations of current software and hardware;

❖ noting any plans for the replacement or enhancement of current SMR computer systems.

The number of county SMRs currently using mainframe and IBM/PC-standard microcomputers for database applications is summarised in Table 4. This ratio has not changed since English Heritage conducted its 1988 survey and none of the SMRs we spoke to had plans to move from its present dependence either on the mainframe computers of its parent body or on a stand-alone PC-based system.

TABLE 4 SMR DATABASE SYSTEMS IN CURRENT USE

	IBM/PC-standard	Mainframe	Total	%
Superfile	16	0	16	34
dBase III & IV/FoxBase	8	1	9	19
SMR-Online	4	0	4	9
SMR-Online/Superfile	2	0	2	4
SMR-Online/North Yorkshire	1	0	1	2
North Yorkshire system	0	3	3	9
Other bespoke systems	2*	9**	11	24
Total	33	13	46	101

* Rescue, Cygnet
** Stairs (2), TPMS Cobol, Mapper, Adabas, Oracle, Ingres, other bespoke (2)

We nevertheless note that a significant number of PC users have recently found it necessary to upgrade their machines to cope with the demands of increasingly large and complicated databases. Those still using older lower-powered machines are aware that the transfer to new and more powerful software systems will require them to replace their hardware in the near future, although several were uncertain about the way in which they will meet the capital cost.

Table 4 also summarises the range of software currently being used by local SMRs for their databases. Key observations that emerge from these data and our discussions with individual SMRs are that:

❖ sixteen of thirty-three PC-using SMRs continue to rely on the English Heritage Superfile package;

❖ four Superfile or dBase SMRs have now converted entirely to SMR-Online;

❖ two further Superfile users and one North Yorkshire system user are in the process of transferring to the interim RCHME SMR-Online system;

❖ ten remaining PC users rely on their own bespoke systems, the majority (8) based on industry-standard dBase relational database software;

❖ three of thirteen mainframe users rely on the specialised database system developed by North Yorkshire County Council;

❖ nine remaining mainframe SMRs use a variety of bespoke systems created for them by the computer departments of their parent local authorities.

TABLE 5 SMR DATABASE SYSTEMS: LEVELS OF SATISFACTION AND PLANS FOR CHANGE

Current system	No. of users	Level of satisfaction (scale: 1–5)	SMRs considering change to			Total
			RCHME	d/Base	Undecided	
Superfile	18	2·76	10	1	4	15
SMR-Online	7	2·14	1			1
d/Base	8	3·62	2		2	4
Other PC*	3	2·67	2			2
Mainframe**	13	3·77	3			3

* Rescue, Cygnet, North Yorkshire

** North Yorkshire (3), Stairs (2), FoxBase, TPMS Cobol, Mapper, Adabas, Oracle, Ingres, other bespoke systems (2)

To find out how well or badly these different database packages are performing, we asked SMR officers to provide a general measure of satisfaction based on a scale of 1 (not at all satisfied) to 5 (very satisfied). From the information summarised in Table 5 it emerges that:

❖ SMRs based on mainframe computer systems are consistently the best satisfied. Of the twelve expressing an opinion, eight gave marks of 4 or 5 and none gave a mark lower than 3.

❖ Amongst PC-based SMRs, the greatest level of satisfaction was expressed by those using bespoke systems based on proprietary dBase software. Six gave marks of 3 or above. In only two cases did a mark of 2 suggest inadequate performance.

❖ The larger group of Superfile users was more varied in its response. Of seventeen who expressed an opinion, more than half gave marks of 3 or above, suggesting that the system still meets their basic needs. The average mark of 2·8 nevertheless confirms repeated comments that the Superfile system is reaching the end of its life and will not provide SMRs with the power and facilities they will need in future.

❖ Of the seven SMRs that are now using the RCHME SMR-Online package, two gave a mark of 4 and another a mark of 3 that imply general satisfaction. Four other SMRs gave a mark of only 1 and told us that they have experienced considerable difficulty with the interim system, which they regard as insufficiently geared to the specialised requirements of an SMR. The RCHME accepts this concern and is shortly to appoint a full-time computer services support post entirely dedicated to SMR-related work. Additionally, the RCHME will be establishing an SMR users group, for those SMRs using RCHME-supplied software.

In a further supporting question we asked SMRs to confirm whether they were planning to replace or upgrade their existing database software. More than half confirmed that this was the case (Table 5):

❖ Of the thirteen mainframe users, three are considering a transfer to the system based on the NAR-Oracle model. The remainder have no plans for change.

❖ Of the thirty-three PC-based SMRs, twenty-two are currently considering the migration of their databases to new operating environments. Thirteen of these expressed a serious interest in the RCHME's proposed replacement for Superfile, while seven others preferred to reserve judgement until they had been able to examine the system's detailed specification. Amongst current Superfile users, just one expressed a specific interest in migrating to a bespoke system based on the proprietary FoxBase relational database package.

3.10 PUBLIC ACCESS TO INFORMATION IN SMRs

Local authority SMRs differ considerably in their policies on the supply of information and advice to outside enquirers. While SMRs housed within museum and library departments tend to have a constitutional responsibility to meet the needs of external users, those located within planning departments and other central administrative sections are often under no such obligation. Instead, they are regarded first and foremost as in-house information systems to which members of the public have no automatic right of access.

In practice, almost all SMRs are willing to provide information and advice to members of the public, both in support of PPG 16 and as a means of promoting public interest and awareness in the historic environment. Individual SMRs nevertheless vary in:

❖ the amounts of time that they can afford to devote to public enquiries;
❖ the kinds of access to SMR information that they allow;
❖ the range of services they offer to outside users;
❖ the extent to which the SMR is actively promoted.

Local SMRs currently spend about 8 per cent of their total time on external enquiries. Reliable figures for actual numbers of external requests for information are not available, but Table 6 confirms the relative proportions that come from six principal categories of user. In almost all counties professional archaeological consultants and contractors form the dominant group, followed by academic researchers and members of the local general public.

Interestingly, use of SMRs by teachers and the media consistently falls low down the list, despite the importance that SMRs claim to attach to their educational and promotional roles. We also note that only seventeen SMRs (35 per cent) maintain a formal userguide to their collections and that only a relatively small proportion actively market and publicise the services of the SMR.

TABLE 6 EXTERNAL SMR USE BY CATEGORY OF CLIENT (1 = MOST FREQUENT; 6 = LEAST FREQUENT)

	Average	Rank
Archaeological consultants	2·18	1
Academic research	2·79	2
General public	2·89	3
Miscellaneous	3·69	4
Education	4·12	5
Media	5·18	6

Very few of the SMRs to whom we spoke allow completely open access to their records. Instead, information is made available through the controlling medium of SMR staff on the grounds that:

❖ SMR records are rarely organised and shelved in a way suited to open access;

❖ manual and computerised records may contain confidential information that cannot be made openly available;

❖ SMR data is liable to misinterpretation by those unfamiliar with its compilation and with the inferential limitations of archaeological evidence;

❖ uncontrolled disclosure of information may threaten the safety of archaeological sites through unauthorised excavation or land development.

During the last five years access to SMR information has become a subject of increasing professional discussion and debate (ACAO 1991, 1993). On the one hand, some county archaeologists have argued that their responsibilities as curators of the local archaeological resource require them to maintain strict control over the supply of information. On the other hand, professional consulting archaeologists have argued that officially compiled heritage records belong within the public domain and should be openly available. We return to the related issues of confidentiality and security of information elsewhere in this report, but would for the present note an urgent need for SMRs to clarify and publish their terms and conditions of public access.

As several county archaeologists pointed out to us, the impact of PPG 16 has not been confined to additional monitoring of planning applications on behalf of district and county authorities. Because PPG 16 encourages consultation in advance of the formal submission of planning applications, local SMRs are having to respond to greatly increased numbers of requests for information from developers and their archaeological consultants. In the case of major developments, the situation is further complicated by the need to provide increasingly robust and detailed data for mandatory Environmental Assessments (EAs) and Environmental Statements.

The majority of SMRs now charge fees for these services. The RCHME nevertheless shares the concern of county archaeologists that the servicing of fee-paying commercial enquiries should not be at the expense of other core SMR functions. Where commercial demand is increasing, local authorities should be willing to reinvest an appropriate proportion of the income back into the SMR rather than into general funds. Unless this is done, SMRs already at saturation point will be unable to respond to the extra demands of PPG 16 and current British and European Environmental Assessment legislation.

3.11
ACADEMIC RESEARCH, EDUCATION AND PUBLICATION

Since SMRs were first established there has been widespread recognition of their value for archaeological and historical research. Accurate quantification is not possible, but we are aware that almost all SMRs actively encourage the use of their records for research on the grounds that the results are likely to:

- increase general understanding of the character and evolution of the local historic environment;
- allow the enhancement of existing SMR site records and descriptions.

SMR staff are themselves frequently engaged in local archaeological research, either as a part of their official duty or in a private capacity. In addition, they maintain close involvement with research work by outside groups that draws in one way or another upon the resources and expertise of the SMR. The RCHME and EH recognise the immense value of this form of collaboration and are concerned that SMR parent bodies should not underestimate its fundamental importance.

The RCHME and EH are equally concerned that SMRs should be encouraged to continue and develop their role in the educational field. Across the country as a whole, the proportions of SMR resources that are devoted to education (3 per cent) and publication (2 per cent) remain small. However, a number of individual counties have given greater emphasis to these functions and report that their modest investment has been rewarded by significantly increased awareness and appreciation of the historic environment. Amongst the educational and promotional initiatives recently taken by SMRs are:

- provision of primary and secondary school teaching materials in response to the requirements of the new National Curriculum;
- production of archaeological leaflets and guidance notes for farmers and landowners;
- assistance with archaeological site interpretation and related visitor facilities;
- publication of popular illustrated books, pamphlets and newsletters on local archaeology;
- active involvement of SMR staff in adult education.

3.12 USE OF SMRs

Table 7 summarises the estimated manpower and financial input to local county SMR user services during 1991.

TABLE 7 SMR INPUT (MAN YEARS AND ESTIMATED COST) TO INFORMATION RETRIEVAL AND RELATED SERVICES AS A PERCENTAGE OF TOTAL SMR RESOURCES, 1991/2

	Core years	%	Contract years	%	All years	%
Planning applications	35.7	30	9.5	12	45.2	22.8
Planning-related enquiries	10.7	9	4.0	5	14.7	7.4
Public and other enquiries	9.5	8	6.3	8	15.8	8.0
Educational services	3.6	3	0.8	1	4.4	2.2
Publication	3.6	3	3.2	4	6.8	3.4
Total	63.1	53	23.8	30	86.9	43.8
Estimated cost	£1.19m		£0.36m		£1.55m	44.8

From this analysis it emerges that:

- SMRs are devoting nearly half of their manpower resources (44 per cent) to the supply of information and advice;
- to meet current demand, the average county SMR now invests an annual 1.9 man years of staff time to user services;

❖ 69 per cent of that time is devoted to planning-related enquiries and the support of PPG 16 at an average cost of 1·3 man years per SMR and a total national cost of £1·07m.

In the Review, SMRs consistently confirmed that the checking of planning applications against the SMR database was their largest single task and the one that on average consumed the greatest proportion (53 per cent) of the time of their core professional staff. There is nevertheless considerable variation in the amount of time that individual SMRs spend on routine development control.

TABLE 8 NUMBERS OF PLANNING APPLICATIONS PROCESSED BY SMRs, 1990

	No. of SMRs	%
>20,000	4	9
15,000–20,000	2	5
10,000–15,000	13	29
5,000–10,000	10	22
<5,000	16	35
Total in sample	45	100

A recent study of the impact of PPG 16 on behalf of English Heritage has shown that 60 per cent of SMRs scan all planning applications submitted within their catchment territory, but that the remainder rely on some preliminary sifting by district planning departments (Pagoda Associates 1992, 10–11). This partly explains the variable response to our own questions about the number of planning applications processed annually by the staff of SMRs (Table 8) and the percentage generating a formal archaeological response (Table 9).

TABLE 9 PERCENTAGE OF PLANNING APPLICATIONS GENERATING AN ARCHAEOLOGICAL RESPONSE

%	No. of SMRs	%
1–2	20	45
3–9	10	23
10–19	6	14
20–29	5	11
>30	3	7
Total in sample	44	100

In their independent study Pagoda Associates concluded that:

❖ a typical county generates 10,000 to 20,000 planning applications a year;
❖ roughly 5 per cent of these (500 to 1,000) require further investigation by the county archaeologist or SMR;
❖ roughly 1 per cent (100 to 200) in turn lead to some kind of positive archaeological intervention.

Pagoda Associates also noted a considerable rise in the number of planning applications requiring the attention of SMR staff since the introduction of PPG 16 in November 1990. Eighty-five per cent of county archaeologists reported an increase in their workload, typically of 25 to 50 per cent, but in some cases of 100 per cent or more (Pagoda Associates 1992, 18).

Significantly, this increase in planning-related casework occurred during a year in which recession is calculated temporarily to have reduced the submission of planning applications by 20 per cent. Our own survey bears out these findings and we agree with the conclusion of Pagoda Associates that 'when the economy recovers county archaeologists will find their workload has increased by 50 to 100 per cent'.

SMRs additionally devote an average 0.6 man years per annum to public enquiries, publication and educational initiatives designed to increase awareness of the historic environment and the resources of the SMR.

3.13 COPYRIGHT AND CHARGING FOR INFORMATION IN SMRs

In the past, local authority SMRs tended to provide advice and information free of charge to internal and external users. More recently, pressure on their limited resources and changing local government policy has encouraged almost all SMRs to look closely at the issue of charging for the supply of their services.

From Table 10 it can be seen that 86 per cent of SMRs now charge fees to professional archaeologists working on behalf of developers and landowners. The number that have extended the principle of charging to other commercial sectors appears to be much smaller, and it is notable that the majority of SMRs have resisted the introduction of search fees for academic users and members of the general public. In the interests of maintaining effective working relationships, SMRs have also been reluctant to charge their district council counterparts for the supply of planning-related information and advice.

TABLE 10 SMRs CHARGING EXTERNAL USERS FOR SERVICES (SAMPLE: 49)

	No. of SMRs	%
Archaeological consultants	42	86
Media	5	10
Other commercial users	5	10
Academic research	3	6
General public	2	4

Many local authorities are still in the process of developing and refining their published policies on charging. We are in addition aware that SMRs are continuing to experiment with alternative approaches to the costing and pricing of their services. During the last two years the ACAO has become aware that a degree of harmonisation between SMRs is needed if outside users are not to be confronted with a bewildering array of conflicting terms and conditions of service.

One of the most serious obstacles to the definition of local and national policies on charging has been the issue of copyright (ACAO 1991, 1993). Because their records are based on information obtained from a wide variety of published and unpublished sources, SMRs have found it exceptionally difficult to define the copyright status of the information contained in their databases. The situation is further complicated by the way in which the cost of compiling and computerising SMR databases has been jointly borne by local authorities, English Heritage and the RCHME. Copyright is an issue that causes parallel difficulties for the RCHME and we return to the subject in our concluding recommendations on the supply of information by SMRs and the NMR.

3.14 Costs

In the course of our review we found it impossible to obtain reliable figures for the total operating cost of the county SMR system in England. This arises from:

- lack of consistency in the way parent bodies apportion the cost of housing and maintaining their SMRs;
- the frequent involvement of county, district and National Park archaeologists and SMR staff in duties only loosely associated with the core functions of SMR enhancement and maintenance;
- the dependence of the majority of SMRs on intermittent external joint-project funding and less easily quantified voluntary assistance and support in kind.

To obtain an approximate picture of current SMR resources we instead asked SMRs to confirm the number of permanent and temporary staff they employed during 1991/2 and the proportion of the cost of their core and supplementary functions that were met respectively by the parent body and external sponsors.

From this information it emerges that the forty-six county and metropolitan authorities contributing to the survey together employed the equivalent of 175 permanent and temporary archaeological staff during 1991, compared with 113 in 1986. Supported by English Heritage funding, this increase reflects the greatly increased workload placed on SMRs by PPG 16, the Monuments Protection Programme and related measures. In addition, the National Trust and National Parks together employed twenty-three staff on SMR-related duties

On the basis of notional salary and overhead costs for permanent and temporary staff (£15k and £12k per person, plus 25 per cent), augmented by firm data on RCHME and EH financial support, the total cost of maintaining the county SMR system during 1991 can thus be roughly computed at £3·01m (Table 11). Of this total amount, £1·95m (65 per cent) supported permanent core staff and the remaining £1·06m personnel employed on short-term contracts.

TABLE 11 ESTIMATED NOTIONAL OPERATING COST (£M) OF COUNTY AND NATIONAL PARK SMRs IN 1991/2

Function	Salary	Overhead	Total	%
Core	1·56	0·39	1·95	65
Supplementary	0·85	0·21	1·06	35
Total	2·41	0·60	3·01	100

According to the information provided to us (Table 12), local authorities now meet 90 per cent of the cost of permanent posts responsible for the basic

TABLE 12 ESTIMATED FUNDING (£M) OF COUNTY AND NATIONAL PARK SMRs IN 1991/2 BY SOURCE

Function	Local authority	English Heritage	RCHME	Developer/Other	Total
Core	1·75 (90%)	0·12 (6%)	0·02 (1%)	0·06 (3%)	1·95
Supplementary	0·27 (25%)	0·36 (34%)	0·24 (23%)	0·19 (18%)	1·06
Total	2·02 (66%)	0·48 (16%)	0·26 (9%)	0·25 (8%)	3·01

curation of their SMRs and the supply of information to internal and external users. However, these same parent bodies cover only 25 per cent of the cost of the period appointments upon which SMRs rely almost exclusively for the development and updating of their record systems. During the later 1970s and 1980s external support for SMR enhancement came from the Inspectorate of Ancient Monuments and English Heritage, augmented to a very significant degree by job-creation funding from the Manpower Services Commission. More recently, however, the sources of outside assistance have begun to broaden and the balance to alter.

By 1991 English Heritage was still the largest external supporter of supplementary SMR projects (34 per cent), but was accompanied by increasingly significant contributions from the RCHME (23 per cent), commercial clients (14 per cent) and other miscellaneous sponsors (4 per cent). In coming years local SMRs anticipate this balance to alter still further. On the one hand, English Heritage contract funding is expected to shift rapidly, in the face of PPG 16, to support of local authority development control functions. On the other hand, RCHME assistance for SMRs is anticipated to increase as the Royal Commission develops its role as the lead body for SMRs and gives increased priority to the completion of an integrated national record of the historic environment. During the next five years SMRs also expect to see a further significant increase in revenue from independent sources, most notably commercial developers and archaeological consultants seeking to meet the requirements of PPG 16.

TABLE 13 SUMMARY ANALYSIS OF MANPOWER INPUTS TO PRINCIPAL AREAS OF SMR ACTIVITY, 1991/2

	Core staff		Contract staff		All	
	years	%	years	%	years	%
Record management	34·4	29	28·4	36	62·8	31·7
Field survey	21·5	18	26·8	34	48·3	24·4
Information supply	63·1	53	23·8	30	86·9	43·9
Total manpower	119·0	100	79·0	100	198·0	100·0

TABLE 14 SUMMARY ANALYSIS OF COST INPUTS TO PRINCIPAL AREAS OF SMR ACTIVITY, 1991/2

	Core staff		Contract staff		All	
	£m	%	£m	%	£m	%
Record management	0·65	29·0	0·43	36·1	1·08	31·5
Field survey	0·40	17·9	0·40	33·6	0·80	23·3
Information supply	1·19	53·1	0·36	30·3	1·55	45·2
Total manpower	2·24	100·0	1·19	100·0	3·43	100·0

To provide a more refined view of the allocation of SMR resources Tables 13 and 14 summarise the manpower and estimated operating cost of all forty-nine English SMRs in terms of their three major areas of functional activity:

- ❖ management and enhancement of the core SMR database;
- ❖ primary field investigation in support of the SMR record;
- ❖ supply of information and advice from the SMR to end users.

This information provides only a generalised model of current SMR resources and their application. The figures are nevertheless likely to be more reliable than any that have been presented previously, having been derived from a section of our questionnaire in which SMRs were asked to confirm actual amounts of permanent and temporary staff time devoted to sixteen distinct categories of work contributing to the three major areas of functional activity. On the basis of this elementary analysis it can be seen that SMRs are able to carry out 53 per cent of their information retrieval and advisory functions through their core permanent staffs, but that they remain heavily dependent on short-term contract staff both for the management and enhancement of the SMR database and for the implementation of associated field survey projects.

4

SCOPE AND CONTENT OF THE NATIONAL AND LOCAL RECORDS

4.1 INTRODUCTION

In this chapter we examine and compare the scope and contents of the National Archaeological Record with that of the forty-six county SMRs. Since SMRs are concerned principally with archaeological sites rather than with buildings, our interest has been directed at the NAR and the 'extended national archaeological record', rather than in the total range of information included in the NMR. We have looked in most detail at the scope and contents of the SMRs, the focus of this Review.

4.2 THE NATIONAL ARCHAEOLOGICAL RECORD: BREADTH OF COVERAGE

The scope of the National Archaeological Record is currently under review and will be extended to cover all archaeological sites of up to 1945 in England and within its territorial waters. What precisely that may mean is described more fully below. At present its scope is essentially that drawn up by the Ordnance Survey Archaeology Division, revised since the transfer of the record in 1983 to take note of particular key RCHME requirements, including notably the extension of the record to include maritime sites and shipwrecks in territorial waters.

Following the previous RCHME Royal Warrant of 1963, it includes all archaeological sites of before 1714. For the period after 1714 in-house recording remains more selective until the current updating programme is completed, but includes all important industrial remains, all scheduled and guardianship monuments, and all Grade I and II* listed buildings. In cases where it is uncertain if a site falls within the sphere of interest, the site is included. Also all sites in county SMRs will be included in the record at a basic index level where these can be transferred digitally. This will add to the NAR a large number of sites of the post-medieval period.

The consistency with which the record has been prepared, since its commencement in 1947, is also one of its greatest strengths in providing quality information at a national or regional level.

4.3 THE NATIONAL ARCHAEOLOGICAL RECORD: DEPTH OF COVERAGE

The depth of coverage for any individual record depends upon the type and level of recording. Staff within the NAR utilise three levels of recording in extracting information from written sources. 'Level 1', the most basic level, recording only location, period and type and sources/bibliography, is used for data derived directly from SMRs and for extensive industrial landscapes, such as the Yorkshire Dales. 'Level 2' is most generally used. Information about the location and character of sites, together with a short description, bibliographic references and cross-references to local SMR and Scheduled Monument record numbers, is compiled with reference to a recording manual that defines the range of mandatory and optional information that should be included. 'Level 3' provides for the same range of information to be recorded, with the addition of a more extensive description and analysis based on a full examination of all available secondary and primary sources.

Through the general use of 'Level 2' recording, adopted since 1985, it is intended that the NAR be brought up to date by concentrating on breadth rather than depth of coverage. The descriptive text which accompanies each record is kept to the minimum essential for national purposes. As the scope of the record is extended this emphasis on breadth rather than depth will become of even greater importance.

Records input by RCHME field survey staff can add a wider range of information, again dependent on the level of recording adopted. 'Level 1' is utilised for the rapid identification of sites, with no measured survey, and only a brief description. 'Level 2' allows for a measured survey generally at 1:2 500, with a fuller description and analysis, together with a wider range of information. 'Level 3' provides for the same range of information to be recorded, but with a larger scale survey together with the addition of a more extensive description and analysis based on a full examination of all available secondary and primary sources.

Records input by RCHME Air Photography Unit staff are similarly at three levels, corresponding to those used by NAR staff. 'Level 1' is the spot location of sites and monuments from air photographs, but with no transcription. The National Mapping Programme utilises 'Level 2' adding a wider range of information. 'Level 3' recording covers the same range of information, but with the addition of larger scale plans and a more extensive description and analysis based on a full examination of all available secondary and primary sources.

4.4 THE NATIONAL ARCHAEOLOGICAL RECORD: CURRENT REVIEW

The RCHME has recently initiated a systematic review of its existing rules and procedures for archaeological recording. This exercise has been prompted by the need to harmonise all RCHME recording procedures following the creation of a single unified NMR database. At the same time it provides a unique opportunity to seek closer correlation between the recording objectives, standards and procedures of the NAR and local SMRs.

Amongst the key issues to be addressed by the RCHME Archaeological Documentation Standards Working Party, in consultation with EH, ACAO and other interested parties, are:

- the range of site types and historic periods that should in future be included within the NAR and SMRs;
- the kinds and levels of information that should in future be recorded respectively by the NMR and local SMRs.

4.5 THE NATIONAL ARCHAEOLOGICAL RECORD: COMPILATION FROM SECONDARY SOURCES

The compilation of the National Archaeological Record follows the system developed since the commencement of the record in 1947, first by the OS and then, since 1983, by the RCHME. The record was based initially on maps, air photographs, original records and literature search in libraries; to reduce travelling costs and make more effective use of staff time, a library has been developed within what is now the NAR. This includes much published material relating to archaeological sites in England; it also includes extensive map collections. All new relevant published literature is systematically searched for references to archaeological sites and investigations. This includes all national and local journals, monographs, festschrifts and publications received by the NAR Library. Additionally, there is exchange of data with local SMRs involved with parallel programmes of archaeological recording and documentation, discussed more fully below.

4.6 THE NATIONAL ARCHAEOLOGICAL RECORD: COMPILATION FROM SURVEY AND RECORDING

The Royal Commission's Air Photography Unit and the Archaeological Field Survey Section both compile records for the NAR from extensive national programmes of primary survey and recording. Records from air photography are derived both from aerial reconnaissance and from transcription work, and represent an input to the NAR added since its transfer to the RCHME in 1983. Records from field survey follow a system developed both from that created by the OS for the field verification of antiquities to be shown on maps and from RCHME practice for the preparation of inventory accounts. Both field survey and air photography programmes now include rapid surveys targeted at parts of the country where the record is particularly weak.

4·7 THE NATIONAL ARCHAEOLOGICAL RECORD: RECORDING MANUALS AND QUALITY CONTROL

Recording systems for NAR, air photography and field survey staff are set out in a series of manuals, linked to computerised recording requirements but incorporating OS, RCHME and DoE systems and standards as appropriate. Quality control systems are implemented in all the RCHME sections to ensure that records are of the desired quality. Input to computer is by controlled vocabulary wherever possible, one important element being the RCHME/EH Archaeological Thesaurus.

4·8 THE NATIONAL ARCHAEOLOGICAL RECORD: SIZE AND RELIABILITY

The NAR currently holds c 150,000 individual site records with at least a further 100,000 awaiting input to the new unified NMR system (Table 15). However, for the purposes of comparison with SMRs, it should be noted that in the NAR there are many site groups which are not broken down into individual units. Most obviously, these include large numbers of Bronze Age round barrows, generally separately recorded in SMRs, but there are many other instances, including some historic towns.

Comparison between the NAR and SMRs has shown that data original to SMRs is biased to post-medieval and/or industrial sites or of sites recorded from air photography, the latter often funded or taken by the RCHME. Systems now in place to ensure that data from RCHME air photographic work is entered to the NAR have been described above. Current recording programmes are intended to ensure that the basic 'Level 1' data for all sites listed in SMRs are recorded in the NAR through agreed programmes of data exchange.

The consistency of compilation since 1947 ensures that the NAR provides reliable coverage of archaeological sites in England. Over 80,000 of the sites included have been checked in the field, generally twice or more. These observations provide a major source of information on the state of England's archaeological resource.

TABLE 15 NUMBER OF NAR ITEMS HELD AT 31 MARCH 1992

	Computer indexed (actual)	Manual (estimate)	Total
Archaeological site records	144,464	c 140,000	284,464
Excavations	25,930		25,930
Survey plans		c 20,000*	c 20,000
Record maps	5,281	c 6,000	11,281
Photographic collection	64,330		64,330
Archive collections held	188	7	195

* Antiquity Models

4·9 THE NATIONAL ARCHAEOLOGICAL RECORD: MAP-BASED RECORDS

Accompanying the computerised site records are some 11,000 Ordnance Survey maps on which are recorded the locations of all sites in the NAR (Table 15). These are prepared to a set of cartographic conventions developed from 1947 onwards, providing a consistent record covering all of England. All areas are covered at 1:10 000. Areas with large numbers of archaeological sites, including many historic towns, are covered at 1:2 500 and 1:1 250.

On OS reprinting the information on the superseded map was formerly transferred by hand to the new edition. The computerised NAR now provides the facility to produce an overlay with all the data from the record automatically plotted, for use over the new printed map. This facility is itself likely to be replaced by a more fully developed geographic information system.

4.10 Other related archaeological records held by the RCHME

The NAR supports its core text record of archaeological sites on the English mainland with the following supplementary indexes:

- a primary record of an estimated 30,000 archaeological sites and wrecks lying in English territorial waters (scheduled for completion in 1995);
- an index of 26,000 archaeological excavations known to have taken place in England, to be expanded to include all archaeological surveys, evaluations and assessments;
- a national index of an estimated 6,000 archaeological archives and collections held in museums, local record offices and elsewhere (scheduled for completion in 1996).

In addition to the creation of a descriptive index of all known archaeological sites and events, the NAR acquires and curates supporting collections of photographs, site plans, written reports and excavation archives. This material is described in detail in *The National Monuments Record: A Guide to the Archive* (RCHME 1990b). In summary, it comprises:

- 20,000 original archaeological survey plans prepared in the course of RCHME field and air photographic survey;
- 64,000 modern and historic photographs of archaeological sites and excavations;
- microfilm copies of 2,500 excavation archives, including much of the work funded by English Heritage and its predecessors;
- microfilm copies of further personal or institutional collections of archaeological papers, drawings and photographs.

4.11 Sites and Monuments Records: breadth of coverage

For the recording of archaeological sites, there are wide variations between SMRs in the upper date limit to which their records run. Of the forty-nine SMRs we consulted, twenty-three (47 per cent) include abandoned man-made structures or deposits of any date if they consider them to be of potential historic interest. Of the remainder, eighteen (37 per cent) terminate their recording at 1945 in line with the RCHME's National Archaeological Record. Eight remaining SMRs maintain intermediate or earlier cut-off dates in the following descending order: Greater London to the date of the most recent listed building; Greater Manchester 1960; Norfolk 1950; Berkshire 1940; Lincolnshire 1750; Cheshire 1700; Leicestershire 1600, and Wiltshire 1500, though most anticipate developing programmes to include all sites up to 1945.

For historic buildings SMRs vary more in what they routinely include and exclude. Only a few have tried to include all listed buildings within the core SMR database; amongst exceptions are Greater London, Bedfordshire, Somerset and the Isle of Wight, while Kent, Hampshire and Cumbria are planning similar exercises. Most SMRs have included standing buildings on a very selective basis, either by confining themselves to Grade I and II* examples recorded by the Ordnance Survey and the NAR, or by focusing on classes of particular local interest or vulnerability.

Several county archaeologists told us that they would like to include a larger number of buildings in their SMR records, but few see this as a major priority. Local responsibility for the overseeing of historic buildings falls to district-level planning departments and conservation officers. Although a number of the latter have begun to compile their own separate databases of historic buildings, the majority rely on the statutory descriptive 'Greenback' lists published by the Department of the Environment.

During the 1970s and early 1980s most county SMRs followed a record structure proposed by the Inspectorate of Ancient Monuments (DoE 1979), itself based substantially on the system developed for the OS National Non-Intensive Record. For twenty-five county SMRs, the adoption of the 'Superfile' database system in the 1980s ensured further standardisation.

There is nevertheless considerable variation in the depth of information that individual SMRs include in their records. A study carried out by English Heritage during 1987/8 (Chadburn 1989) showed that only six SMRs regularly used all of the twenty-five standard information fields available to them. Most had instead concentrated on core data about the location and character of sites and had given lower priority to supporting information on their environmental setting, ownership, condition and protected status. From our own study we conclude that this remains the case. We were also interested to note that thirty-five (71 per cent) SMRs have found it necessary to create additional data fields to meet their own local requirements; a trend that suggests increasing differences in the kinds of information now needed by English Heritage and local authorities.

4.12 SITES AND MONUMENTS RECORDS: DEPTH OF COVERAGE

When county SMRs were being established in the 1970s and 1980s the range and structure of their data was defined broadly by the requirements of the AM 107 recording form. During subsequent computerisation of their manual records SMRs tended to adopt a wider variety of data structure and standards. At one level this variation resulted from differing local perceptions of the aims of computerisation; at another it was influenced by the choice of computer hardware and software currently available. As a result of this phase of independent parallel development, comparison of data held in different local SMRs has become more difficult, as has the exchange of digital information between SMRs and with the NMR and English Heritage.

There is also a variation in the data structure adopted by SMRs. Individual records refer variously to single archaeological sites, single land parcels containing archaeological sites, or single pieces of received information about archaeological sites. Within these broad groupings there are further variations, often introduced to avoid the problems encountered in recording complex landscapes and urban areas; in 1987–8, twenty-seven SMRs used component records, though these varied greatly in structure and content (Chadburn 1989, 10–12).

4.13 SITES AND MONUMENTS RECORDS: DATA STANDARDS AND STRUCTURE

All but one of the SMRs consulted during this survey hold copies of archaeological record cards taken from the national record, before 1983 from the OS, since then from the RCHME. During the 1970s and 1980s almost all counties used the OS record as the basis of their new SMRs. Not all counties obtained copies of the record maps, and not all obtained copies of cards prior to 1983 directly from the OS. There is thus some variation in the extent to which the information held in the national record has been transmitted in its entirety to the SMRs.

From this starting point, most have amplified their coverage through consultation of a variety of other existing sources of published and unpublished information. To obtain a picture of the relative thoroughness with which secondary sources have been trawled for information we asked SMRs to confirm the use they had made of three principal categories of material: published books and journals; unpublished national indexes, and unpublished archives.

4.14 SITES AND MONUMENTS RECORDS: COMPILATION FROM SECONDARY SOURCES

Table 16 shows that SMRs have given priority to obtaining information from the OS/NAR record of archaeological sites, from literature search and from county record offices. Potential sources of information that have been examined by much smaller proportions of SMRs are the published volumes of the Place Name Society, the Public Record Office in London, the national index of archaeological excavations maintained by the NMR, the collected records of the Medieval Village Research Group (MVRG) held in the NMR and the NMR Buildings Index.

TABLE 16 NUMBER AND PERCENTAGE OF SMRs SYSTEMATICALLY OR SELECTIVELY CONSULTING SECONDARY SOURCES OF PUBLISHED AND UNPUBLISHED INFORMATION

	Consulted	%	Not consulted	%
PUBLICATIONS				
Local journals	46	94	3	6
Victoria County History	43	88	6	12
National journals	38	78	11	22
Place name volumes	26	53	23	47
UNPUBLISHED INDEXES				
OS/NAR record cards	43	88	6	12
NMR Excavation Index	21	43	28	57
MVRG index cards	13	27	36	73
NMR Buildings Index	5	10	44	90
UNPUBLISHED ARCHIVES				
Local record office	38	78	11	22
Local museum records	37	76	12	24
Air photographs	33	67	16	33
Public Record Office	16	33	33	67

In addition, several SMR officers have noted:

❖ that their initial trawling of published and unpublished sources was often necessarily rapid and selective rather than exhaustive;
❖ that lack of resources has frequently prevented them from searching subsequent publications or more recently collected archival material.

TABLE 17 SMR INPUT (MAN YEARS AND CASH EQUIVALENT) TO THE MAINTENANCE AND ENHANCEMENT OF THE CORE DATABASE AS A PROPORTION OF TOTAL MANPOWER AVAILABILITY, 1991

	Core years	%	Contract years	%	All years	%
Maintenance:						
computerised record	8.3	7	7.1	9	15.4	7.8
Enhancement:						
computerised record	10.7	9	12.6	16	23.3	11.7
Maintenance:						
manual record	7.1	6	2.4	3	9.5	4.8
Enhancement:						
manual record	8.3	7	6.3	8	14.6	7.4
Total (manpower)	34.4	29	28.4	36	62.8	31.7
Estimated cost	£0.65m		£0.43m		£1.08m	31.5

The amount of time devoted by SMR staff to the maintenance and enhancement of their computerised databases, supporting manual indexes and record maps is summarised in Table 17, together with an outline estimate of the cost of this work. From these data it can be seen that SMRs are currently devoting a third of their manpower resources to the management of the core SMR database at an overall estimated cost of £1·08m. Of this input, some 60 per cent (37·9 man years, £0·65m) is directed specifically towards enhancement of existing manual and computerised records of archaeological sites and historic buildings.

4·15 Sites and Monuments Records: compilation from primary survey and recording

In addition to scanning published and unpublished documentary sources, all SMRs enhance their records on the basis of primary field observation and investigation. This information is acquired in a number of different ways:

- reports of chance finds and discoveries;
- information from field survey, excavation and other kinds of investigation carried out by the RCHME, EH, professional archaeological units and local societies;
- programmes of field survey and site inspection carried out by the SMR itself.

Reports of accidental finds remain a key source of information and demonstrate the fundamental value of an effective local intelligence network. SMRs also confirm that close working relationships with local museums, archaeological and historical societies, universities and professional archaeological units allow them to be rapidly informed about the results of current field investigation. Slightly less satisfactory has been the flow of information from organisations operating from outside the SMR's catchment area. A number of SMRs have in particular drawn attention to the need for more effective communication with the RCHME about the results of recent programmes of field survey and aerial reconnaissance.

TABLE 18 SMR INPUT (MAN YEARS AND ESTIMATED COST) TO SURVEY-RELATED FUNCTIONS AS A PERCENTAGE OF TOTAL MANPOWER AVAILABILITY, 1991

	Core years	%	Contract years	%	All years	%
Site inspection	11.9	10	4.7	6	16.6	8.4
Excavation	2.4	2	7.1	9	9.5	4.8
Post-excavation/survey	1.2	1	7.9	10	9.1	4.6
Aerial survey	2.4	2	3.1	4	5.5	2.8
Archaeological field survey	2.4	2	2.4	3	4.8	2.4
Architectural field survey	1.2	1	1.6	2	2.8	1.4
Total (manpower)	21.5	18	26.8	34	48.3	24.4
Estimated cost	£0.40m		£0.40m		£0.80m	23.3
Total less site inspection	9.6	8	22.2	28	31.8	16.0
Estimated cost	£0·18m		£0·33m		£0·50m	14.7

The proportion of their own resources that SMRs devote to primary field investigation is variable. Some rely almost entirely on work carried out by other organisations while others have developed their own in-house programmes of ground-based and air photographic survey. Apart from site visits directly associated with planning casework, primary field investigation tends to be supported by external funding, most notably in the form of contracts and grant aid from EH or the RCHME. Table 18 shows that SMRs currently devote a fifth of their core manpower and just over a third of their contract staff time to survey-related activities. If planning-related site inspection is removed from these figures, the total annual SMR input to primary survey and excavation falls to 31.8 man years (£0.5m; 16 per cent of total manpower resource).

4.16 Recording manuals and quality control

Forty-two (86 per cent) SMRs now maintain some form of written guide for staff adding information to the SMR. In addition, all SMRs use formal glossaries of the words and terms used in their database records. This widespread adoption of formal recording manuals and systems of vocabulary control confirms the importance that SMRs now attach to consistency in the compilation of their records. Elsewhere in this report we look in greater detail at the linked issues of data and information standards. For the present it nevertheless deserves to be noted that:

- ❖ SMRs have so far made little effort to harmonise their own recording manuals with those of other counties or with the NAR recording manual. While each SMR will inevitably have certain specialised needs of its own, there would seem to be considerable room for shared investment and co-operation in this field.
- ❖ Although all forty-nine SMRs maintain some form of vocabulary control, only six employ systems that are consonant with the RCHME/EH Thesaurus of Archaeological Site Types (2nd edition, 1992).
- ❖ Although the majority of SMRs have formal procedures for checking the technical validity of their computerised data, most still rely on less formal methods for confirming the academic integrity of information entered into SMRs. We have not been able to explore this issue in detail, but suggest that it may be a legitimate subject for further consultation and review by the RCHME and SMRs.

4.17 Size and reliability of SMR databases

In 1984 English Heritage attempted to quantify the national stock of known archaeological sites. For the purpose of this census individual SMRs were asked to estimate the number of records that they expected to hold at the end of their primary rounds of compilation and computerisation. The resulting total of 630,000 compared with the 12,500 sites then registered as Scheduled Ancient Monuments and the 150,000 monuments listed in the NAR, the last including many groups of sites broken down by SMRs into component parts (DoE 1984).

In presenting the figure of 630,000 sites, English Heritage was at pains to emphasise a critical methodological factor that still applies. This concerns the varied ways in which SMRs define and record their 'sites'. Whereas some are prepared to register large numbers of separate but neighbouring structures within a single record, others list each feature or find spot as a 'site' in its own right. In recent years the issue of site definition has been the subject of extensive professional debate and has still to be fully resolved. For the present, it has to be recognised that the simple counting of SMR records is liable to provide a distorted view of the actual density of archaeological remains in different parts of the country.

For the purpose of this present Review we followed the example of the 1984 English Heritage survey by asking SMRs to confirm the number of records that they currently hold under each of five main historical headings: prehistoric,

Roman, medieval, post medieval and uncertain. From the information provided to us it emerges that:

- The forty-nine English SMRs taking part in the survey together hold 638,160 records; a figure close to the 630,000 projected in *England's Archaeological Resource* (DoE 1984).
- This crude total includes 30,000 records held by the National Trust and the North York Moors National Park that duplicate records contained in the parallel county SMRs. Deduction of this figure reduces the crude national total to 608,160.
- Figures for county SMRs include up to 40,000 archaeological sites and 15,500 listed buildings not yet entered into the machine-retrievable database.

On the basis of the information available to us, reliable quantification of the numbers of archaeological sites now recorded in SMRs remains impossible. The situation is exacerbated because:

- Only twenty-five of England's forty-six county SMRs can provide accurate counts of their total numbers of SMR records, the remainder depending on rough estimates to the nearest hundred, thousand or ten thousand. In our view these unsupported estimates may inflate the actual total of records by up to 30,000.
- Twelve of these SMRs were additionally unable to provide a breakdown of their sites by period.
- The legitimate recording of some sites under more than one period heading will in some counties have led to double-scoring. In the absence of firm evidence we suggest provisionally that multiple recording may have inflated the national total of spatially distinct sites by as much as 10 per cent, or 60,000.
- The form of our questions to SMRs prevented our determining the proportion of sites that are in practice standing historic buildings. A useful insight to this issue is provided by an analysis of 161,344 SMR site records (approximately a quarter of the national total) carried out in 1990 on behalf of the ACAO (Lang 1990, Fig 2). This confirmed (Table 19) that 18·6 per cent of the sampled records related to listed buildings. Repeated across the country, this ratio would yield a total of 113,000 listed buildings amongst the 608,157 records currently contained within local SMRs.
- A further significant observation is that more than a third (34·7 per cent) of the records in Lang's sample related to find spots rather than to archaeological sites with known structural remains.

TABLE 19 SELECTIVE SAMPLE OF SMR RECORDS BY SITE TYPE

	Records	%
Find spots	56,002	34·7
Listed buildings	29,987	18·6
Earthworks	25,476	15·8
Cropmarks	17,992	11·2
Industrial sites	8,427	5·2
Urban deposits	5,153	3·2
Ancient woods and hedges	490	0·3
Other (unidentified)	17,817	11·0
Total	161,344	100·0

(Source: Lang 1990)

Our overall conclusions based on the limited data available to us are:

❖ that the RCHME is concerned at the number of SMRs that seem unable to provide accurate figures for the total numbers of monuments recorded in their SMRs and the breakdown of those sites by structural type and historical period;

❖ that the methods of scoring used in this and earlier surveys may exaggerate by a half the real number of archaeological sites listed in SMR databases. In our opinion the future concordance of existing SMR and NAR records and the exclusion of listed buildings will show the true total of archaeological sites to lie closer to 300,000. Only when the RCHME has completed the SMR/NAR concordance through data exchange will national quantification be possible.

The above discussion relates only to those sites of archaeological interest that have already been recorded by county SMRs. From our discussions with individual county archaeologists, the ADAO and English Heritage, and from our own observations, it emerges that:

❖ many SMRs remain deficient in their primary recording for certain periods (most notably the industrial and modern) and geographical areas (most notably historic town centres and the maritime zone) and will need to extend the breadth of their coverage if they are to constitute a reliable database across the whole spectrum of the historic environment;

❖ the majority of SMRs are aware of a need, for the purposes of effective archaeological management, to increase the depth of the information that they hold about particular categories of site and for geographical areas of exceptional significance or vulnerability. In particular, it is widely recognised that SMRs will in future need to give much greater priority to monitoring and recording the changing physical condition of monuments.

TABLE 20 SMR PRIORITIES FOR RECORD ENHANCEMENT

	No. of SMRs	%
Depth of archaeological record	42	85
Depth of architectural record	36	73
Breadth of archaeological record	30	61
Breadth of architectural record	28	57

From Table 20 it can be seen that the highest priority of most SMRs is more detailed recording of the archaeological sites and buildings about which they already have some basic information. At the same time more than half recognised that they still have a need to increase the breadth of their primary archaeological and architectural databases. In terms of primary archaeological recording the most frequently cited areas of weakness are the fields of industrial, maritime and First and Second World War archaeology (Table 21). Amongst other more specific areas, in which individual SMRs acknowledge their coverage deficient (in both depth and breadth) in relation to current and anticipated demands for information, are:

❖ earthworks in woodland, ancient pasture and upland moorland
❖ sites recorded by aerial photography
❖ relict prehistoric and medieval landscapes
❖ sub-surface deposits in historic towns and villages

- historic parks, gardens and managed woodlands
- historic buildings, including schools and churches
- palaeo-environmental evidence
- stray finds recorded in museum records
- place name evidence

TABLE 21 PRIORITIES FOR ENHANCEMENT OF THE BREADTH OF SMR ARCHAEOLOGICAL COVERAGE

	No. of SMRs	%
Maritime sites (sample: 23 coastal counties)	21	91
Industrial archaeology	43	88
20th-century military sites	35	71
Other	31	63

4.18 MAP-BASED RECORDS

For purposes of archaeological development control all SMRs maintain collections of maps showing the location and extent of sites recorded in their SMR databases. The quality and format of these record maps is very varied.

Most SMRs now maintain their primary mapped record at a scale of 1:10 000, although a significant proportion continue to use the now defunct 1:10 560 scale as their standard. In addition to their primary 1:10 000 map coverage, a number of SMRs maintain larger scale 1:2 500 and 1:1 250 record maps for historic urban areas with high densities of archaeological sites and listed buildings.

The majority of SMRs now record archaeological sites on translucent overlays to standard Ordnance Survey map sheets. Alternatively, information is annotated directly on to the map sheets themselves. In some cases sites of all periods and categories are included on a single record map or overlay sheet; in others separate maps and overlays are used for different classes of information.

More varied still is the manner in which different SMRs depict sites on their primary record maps. Some limit their cartographic depiction to simple dots and crosses marking the centres of sites; others include outer banding lines to give a better indication of the extent of the area of archaeological significance, while a third category attempt systematically to depict the shape and size of each separate archaeological structure.

Throughout the last fifteen years a topic of particular importance to local SMRs has been the mapping of the many thousands of archaeological sites discovered by aerial photography. With initial financial support from English Heritage and the more recent assistance of the RCHME, most counties in England now possess a basic mapped record of sites discovered and recorded from the air. However, it has been recognised that much of this material will in the near future require systematic enhancement and updating if it is to serve the needs of the MPP and PPG 16. Towards that end the RCHME has recently announced its support of a ten-year national programme designed to bring existing SMR air photographic transcription up to the necessary standards of accuracy and consistency.

In the course of this Review it has been noted that SMRs, the RCHME and English Heritage are each currently involved in the production of record maps for their own particular purposes. We return elsewhere to the issue of potential duplication of effort (Chapter 6). For the present it is sufficient to note that no attempt has thus far been made to encourage the development of common standards for SMR and national map-based recording and that the lack of such standards may in future severely limit the application of

Geographic Information System technology to the shared benefit of SMRs, the NMR and English Heritage.

4.19 OTHER NON-COMPUTERISED RECORDS HELD BY SMRs

In addition to their core computerised and map-based records, local SMRs collect a range (Table 22) of supporting information and material falling into the following broad categories:

- Books, journals, maps and other conventionally published material required for reference and research, including official gazetteers of scheduled monuments and listed buildings.
- Copies of Ordnance Survey archaeological record cards and other unpublished public records compiled or held by the NMR.
- Limited circulation reports of archaeological and architectural surveys, evaluations and other forms of primary and secondary investigation.
- Unpublished archaeological plans, drawings, field notes, photographic negatives and other original archive material.
- Collections of aerial photographs.

TABLE 22 SUPPORTING INDEXES AND SOURCES OF INFORMATION TYPICALLY HELD BY LOCAL SMRs

	No. of SMRs	%
Scheduled Monument lists	49	100
NAR (OS) record cards	48	98
Collections of air photographs	45	92
EH Register of Parks and Gardens	39	80
NMR Excavation Index	35	71
DoE lists of historic buildings	32	65
CBA Industrial Monuments Survey	8	16
Medieval Settlement Research Group record cards	6	12

Only a limited number of SMRs, mainly those attached to local authority museum and library departments, operate under the terms of a defined collecting policy. Published and unpublished material instead tends to be acquired on a relatively informal basis, depending on perceived local need and opportunity.

4.20 UPDATING THE NATIONAL ARCHAEOLOGICAL RECORD AND SITES AND MONUMENTS RECORDS THROUGH DATA EXCHANGE

It will be evident that both the NAR and SMRs can be updated by access to one another's records. In 1987 agreement was reached between the RCHME and the Association of County Archaeological Officers regarding the routine exchange of archaeological information, between the NAR and county SMRs, following a pilot data-transfer exercise with the Somerset SMR. This information is at present transferred largely in digital form.

Between 1987 and October 1992 the NAR had completed primary data-exchange exercises with twelve county SMRs and was actively implementing or planning sixteen others. In this same period the NAR had supplied substantial amounts of data to eighteen SMRs. Although not all in digital form this data included information for eight complete counties, in four instances forming the basis for a new SMR utilising the RCHME SMR-Online software.

Transfer of digital data has so far been hampered by the diversity of computer systems between which data has to be transferred. It has been further exacerbated by the varying data standards used by different county SMRs. In the majority of cases these problems can be overcome, but often only with considerable difficulty. In the light of this experience the RCHME and the ACAO have jointly recognised that effective exchange of information will in future depend on the acceptance of the framework of core data standards currently being developed by a joint RCHME/ACAO working party. This subject is discussed further in the concluding chapter.

5

THE ROLES OF THE NMR AND SMRS

5.1

THE EXTENDED NATIONAL RECORD

The revised Royal Warrant (1992) requires the RCHME to provide the 'basic national record of the archaeological and historical environment ... all buildings, sites and ancient monuments of archaeological, architectural and historical interest in England'. This record is concerned not only with the results of the Royal Commission's own survey and investigation, but with information from all sources.

It is neither feasible nor desirable for all of this information to be held centrally within the NMR. In future the national heritage database should be seen as an extended record, some elements of which will be curated centrally by the NMR and EH (in the case of the registers of Scheduled Monuments and Historic Parks); other elements will be curated locally by SMRs. In this extended record, the principal role of the NMR will be:

- to provide the national index to sites and monuments described and documented in greater detail by SMRs;
- to provide information on the archaeological and historic environment to national and local government, government agencies, other organisations and the general public, particularly at a national or regional level;
- to provide information on the forms, level and status of information about the historic environment collected and held by central government agencies, local SMRs and all other relevant bodies;
- to curate the results of the Royal Commission's own investigative work;
- to serve as the national archive for documents, photographs and drawings relating to the historic built environment of England;
- to establish and provide national standards for surveying, recording and record curating.

The future organisation, scope and content of this extended national record is discussed further in the next chapter.

5.2

RCHME RESPONSIBILITY FOR THE OVERSIGHT OF LOCAL SITES AND MONUMENTS RECORDS

The revised Royal Warrant also charges the RCHME with 'responsibility for the oversight of local Sites and Monuments Records'. This should be achieved through various means, including this Review, improved liaison procedures, the provision of training and making available appropriate SMR database software and support.

5.3

IMPROVED LIAISON PROCEDURES

More effective liaison and communication is required between the RCHME and SMRs. We recommend that the RCHME, ACAO and ADAO examine the existing system of regional SMR Working Parties to ensure that these provide an effective permanent channel of communication between SMR officers and the RCHME together with EH.

5.4

TRAINING AND SPECIALIST SUPPORT FOR SMRs

If local SMRs are to fulfil the roles recommended in this report it is essential that their staff have access to appropriate professional training and technical support. It has emerged that SMRs at present receive only limited resources for formal staff training from the parent bodies. It is in addition apparent that many

SMRs depend heavily on external technical support for the maintenance of their computerised databases and for the undertaking of specialised archaeological and architectural survey.

On the assumption of its responsibility for oversight of SMRs the RCHME announced that it intended to give high priority to ensuring that individual SMRs receive the training and specialist support that they require. In appropriate circumstances this support will be provided financially or in kind by the Royal Commission itself, but in other situations the RCHME will argue that it is the proper and legitimate responsibility of the parent local authority.

Current arrangements for the secondment of SMR staff to the RCHME for practical in-service training will be developed and expanded. Priority will in the first instance be given to training in the fields of database administration, collections management, archaeological field survey and aerial photography. Depending on demand, the RCHME may also arrange courses of formal instruction in these and related fields.

Subject to operational capacity, the RCHME will undertake to provide professional advice and guidance in support of the planning and implementation of archaeological and architectural survey and recording projects initiated by SMRs.

5.5 RCHME SUPPORT FOR SMR COMPUTER SYSTEMS

The RCHME is committed to making available an entirely new database system that will meet the additional functional requirements of SMRs, while remaining compatible with the structure and standards of the newly unified NMR. Already seven SMRs are using a software package based on the existing computerised NAR. The new software should include provision for the data structure and standards for urban SMRs shortly to be finalised by the RCHME and EH.

Funding for the development of this new system has been made available from the DoE's supplementary 1992/3 grant to the RCHME for SMR enhancement. The new system is being designed in close consultation with SMR users and is scheduled for delivery in 1993. Thereafter the package will be available to any SMR wishing to adopt it, subject to that SMR's willingness to conform to the core data and information standards agreed by the ACAO, English Heritage and the RCHME. Training and technical support will be provided to SMRs adopting the replacement system. In appropriate circumstances the RCHME will contribute to the cost of migrating existing computerised data to the new system at agreed points in a three-year implementation period running from 1993/4–1995/6. The RCHME plans to establish and co-ordinate a national SMR Information Technology Users Group to succeed the former Superfile Users Group. It also intends that its support for the new system should be ongoing, allowing subsequent releases of the software to reflect the developing operational requirements of local SMRs, including those associated with the application of GIS technology.

5.6 THE ROLE OF SMRs

SMRs now provide indispensable information to those providing archaeological advice in local authority planning departments, in accordance with the requirements of PPG 16. They also provide information for both local authority strategic planning, particularly in relation to the development of policies for construction, minerals, agricultural development and tourism, and to private developers, statutory undertakers and government departments contemplating development work.

English Heritage has recognised local SMRs as the major source of information for its Monuments Protection Programme. The RCHME recognises that SMRs are an important component of the extended national record, playing a key role in the enhancement and updating of the record for their areas.

5.7
STAFFING LEVELS OF SMRs

When asked to anticipate their future resources, SMRs confirmed that their complement of core staff is planned to rise by a national average of 12 per cent by 1996/7. The RCHME and English Heritage consider this is a conservative planning figure that takes insufficient account of the depth and breadth of information that SMRs are likely to be asked to supply in response to the developing impact of PPG 16 and European Environmental Assessment legislation.

Although a significant proportion of the cost may subsequently be recovered from fees charged to developers and archaeological consultants, we recommend that local authorities should plan for a 50 per cent to 100 per cent increase in planning-led SMR casework in the five-year period 1992/3 to 1996/7.

5.8
THE LOCATION OF SMRs WITHIN LOCAL AUTHORITIES

Notwithstanding their close association with the planning process, only half of England's forty-six county and metropolitan SMRs are now housed within planning departments. The location of SMRs within other local authority departments, or outside the local authority altogether, poses some important questions:

- Does the county authority remain the best base for the operation of an SMR or is there a case for the transfer of SMRs to independent management?
- Is the present variable pattern acceptable or may there be a case for greater conformity in the way in which SMRs are housed within their parent bodies?
- If there is a case for greater uniformity, will local and national needs be best served by locating SMRs within planning departments or elsewhere within the local authority?

In the view of the RCHME and EH the housing of SMRs within local authorities has proved a successful and effective arrangement that assures the open supply of information and advice to both official and public users. In the course of this Review EH and the majority of county archaeologists and SMR officers confirmed that they were strongly in favour of the maintenance of the SMR as a constituent part of the planning department. In support of their case it was argued that an intimate relationship with the planning process is the best means of monitoring threats to the historic environment and of ensuring the proper consideration of archaeological priorities in both tactical and strategic planning decisions. By contrast, some other SMR officers argued that the location of the SMR within the local museums or library service offered better scope for impartiality, greater constitutional stability and increased freedom to supply information and advice to the public as well as to internal clients.

Each of these arguments carries weight and from our observations we conclude that neither model has overriding practical advantages. While SMRs located in planning departments certainly benefit from a close working relationship with the general planning process, our discussions have shown that SMRs located elsewhere within the local authority system have invariably been able to evolve effective lines of communication with their planning counterparts.

5.9
THE IMPARTIALITY OF ARCHAEOLOGICAL ADVICE TO LOCAL AUTHORITIES

Through PPG 16 the local SMR is recognised as the standard public source of information and advice for those contemplating development work. At the same time, the staff of SMRs are closely involved in the assessment of planning applications, both in their role as advisers to district planning departments and through their line management responsibility to the county archaeologist. In turn, the position of some county archaeologists is further complicated by their simultaneous responsibility for the management of professional archaeological field units.

It has been suggested that this situation may give rise to a conflict of interest between the role of the SMR as an impartial provider of information and advice; its duty to support the policies of the local authority and its wider responsibility to the protection of the historic landscape. In the independent view of EH, the high professional standards adopted by individual SMR officers, county archaeologists and their counterparts in districts and National Parks have thus far prevented any serious compromise between competing internal, external and professional obligations. The potential for such conflicts of interest nevertheless remains.

On this and related issues we recommend that:

- Local authorities should publish guidelines that clearly define the constitutional position and responsibilities of any SMR maintained as a source of public and internal advice and information.
- Local authorities should ensure that the impartiality of the SMR is not compromised by any management relationships that may exist between the SMR and the county, district or National Park archaeology officer, especially where that officer also serves as the director of a professional archaeological unit.
- Local authorities should not obtain information or advice from SMRs maintained by organisations operating simultaneously as commercial archaeological contractors or developer consultants unless safeguards ensuring impartiality are in place.

5.10 NATIONAL PARKS

The recent review of the National Parks has recommended that for each there be available an archaeological database (Countryside Commission 1991). We recommend that wherever possible this be achieved by networking to the existing county SMR(s) or the unified NMR, failing that by data transfer.

5.11 DISTRICT AUTHORITIES

Although satisfactory arrangements for the exchange of information and advice have been established between the majority of districts and their parent counties, there remain situations in which co-operation falls below the level necessary for the reliable and effective implementation of PPG 16 by the district authority (Pagoda Associates 1992, 4.1.3). We recommend that EH should continue to monitor and report upon the effectiveness of relationships between county SMRs and district planning authorities.

Urban databases are to be established in upwards of thirty historic towns. We recommend that these urban databases should form part of the extended national record, so as to avoid the proliferation of duplicate record systems and to serve as the means by which the national record is updated. If networked to the unified NMR, the urban databases would in turn have immediate computer access to RCHME information particularly relevant to urban archaeology, including archaeological excavations and architectural data. In setting up new urban databases the RCHME and EH should ensure that the relationship between the new record and the existing county SMR is clearly defined.

The Association of District Archaeological Officers acknowledges that all district authorities should have access to an SMR. We recommend that, with the exception of historic towns, this be achieved through links to the existing county SMR or to the extended unified NMR, either by data transfer or by networking.

5.12 HISTORIC BUILDINGS

Several SMRs already hold records of historic buildings. In view of the forthcoming feasibility study instigated by the DNH on the national computerisation of the lists, which will be completed by the end of the 1992/3 financial year, we recommend that SMRs do not embark upon a programme of enhancement of these records.

5.13 THE STATUS OF SMRs

Because of their dependence on the local SMR system, the RCHME and English Heritage have each expressed concern about the constitutional position of SMRs within their parent local authorities. Whereas county councils in England are legally obliged to maintain county record offices, their maintenance of accessible SMRs remains voluntary. In the view of the RCHME and EH, this situation provides insufficient protection for the archaeological heritage.

We therefore recommend that:

- The Department of National Heritage and the Department of the Environment should jointly issue an advisory note defining the core requirements of a local SMR and the terms under which it should be curated.
- The maintenance of an SMR should become a formally recognised responsibility of every county council or unitary planning authority in England.
- The cost of maintaining that SMR should be formally included within the Standard Spending Assessment (SSA) for the local authority in question.

5.14 LOCAL GOVERNMENT REORGANISATION: COUNTY, DISTRICT AND NATIONAL PARK SMRs

It is probable that the recently established Local Government Commission for England will in some parts of the country recommend replacement of the current two-tier system of county and district authorities with a simplified system of unitary authorities.

The RCHME recognises that the creation of unitary authorities could help to overcome difficulties presented by the current division of responsibilities for the management of the historic environment between county and district authorities:

- There are potential benefits from a closer relationship of SMRs, currently maintained at county level, with development control functions currently performed at district level.
- There are opportunities afforded for linkage of archaeological and architectural advisory functions currently performed by county archaeological officers and district conservation officers.
- There are opportunities for the development of SMRs providing systematic local coverage of both archaeological sites and historic buildings.

At the same time, very careful consideration will need to be given to the efficiency and cost-effectiveness of SMRs if the current network of forty-six shire and metropolitan counties is replaced by a larger number of unitary local authorities of varying sizes. The most critical causes of concern in this area are:

- the initial cost of dividing and reconstructing existing SMRs to meet the needs of new geographical territories;
- the ongoing cost of staffing an expanded network of SMRs each responsible for a smaller geographical area;
- the loss of regional perspective in the recording and management of the historic environment;
- the difficulties of guaranteeing effective national data standards and data exchange agreements within an expanded network of SMRs;
- the loss or fragmentation of essential knowledge and experience built up amongst existing SMR staff.

In the event of local government reorganisation SMR coverage could be provided in a number of different ways, depending on the size and historical importance of individual local authority areas.

The paramount concern of the RCHME and English Heritage will be the existence of a firmly constituted and securely resourced unitary system of national SMR coverage. We recommend that the Local Government Commission for England should:

- give explicit attention to the protection and continuity of the services provided by existing SMRs;
- take note of the shared view of the RCHME and EH that provision of the necessary range of SMR services and expertise may not always be practicable within an area significantly smaller than a traditional rural county or large historic town;
- in appropriate circumstances recommend the retention or amalgamation of existing county SMRs as a specialist umbrella of regional support to groups of constituent local authorities;
- ensure that any new local planning authority is required to maintain or secure permanent access to an appropriately staffed SMR;
- give the strongest possible encouragement to the inclusion of SMR services within the Standing Spending Assessment (SSA) for any newly created local authority.

5.15 Greater London SMR

The SMR for Greater London (GLSMR) is held by EH. We recommend that EH and the RCHME discuss the relationship of the GLSMR with the NMR with a view to future networking of information. This would eliminate the extra costs arising from much of the same archaeological and architectural data being held by two national organisations.

5.16 Copyright and charging for information in the NMR and SMRs

In view of the importance and complexity of these issues we recommend that the RCHME, EH, ACAO, ADAO and other relevant parties should jointly discuss whether it is possible to develop an agreed policy for issues of copyright, ownership and charging, for the organisations contributing to the extended national record.

5.17 Costs of future SMR provision

In the view of the RCHME and EH the cost of the core tasks of managing an existing SMR record and providing a responsive service of advice and information retrieval to the parent local authority, developers and other outside users should remain a charge on the parent local authority, and should not normally be met from central government funds. Where EH or the RCHME require access to the core services of an SMR on behalf of central government, it is recommended that these should be provided either free of charge on the basis of standing *quid pro quo* agreements or as the subject of specific contractual arrangements.

In the updating and revision of the primary SMR database it has been noted that SMRs depend heavily on funding from the RCHME, EH and other external sponsors for the essential enhancement of their records. Moreover, the forty-nine SMRs we questioned expect this already inadequate resource to decline by 40 per cent over the next five years as EH progressively withdraws financial support for the creation and enhancement of local SMRs. In this same period English Heritage will, however, be continuing to support posts concerned with PPG 16 development control.

The RCHME and EH consider that the periodic revision of an SMR database is properly a responsibility of the SMR parent body, on the grounds that the

Town and Country Planning General Development Order (GDO) and PPG 16 require local authorities to have access to up-to-date local records of the historic environment.

It is at the same time important to recognise that a number of SMRs remain incomplete in their coverage of certain categories of sites and monuments, most notably those of the post-medieval and industrial periods. In addition, many of their existing core records require refinement and validation if they are to serve as a reliable source of information for statutory development control and for consultation by outside users. An accurate forecast of the cost of bringing England's forty-six county and National Park SMRs to a uniform standard will not be available until detailed qualitative audits have been carried out of the contents of individual SMRs and relevant components of the NMR. Moreover, the cost of enhancement is likely to vary significantly from one SMR to another, depending on past levels of investment and differing spheres of interest. In some counties an input of 2 to 5 man years is likely to be sufficient, but in others backlogs of unaccessioned information and requirements for further primary investigation may require the investment of up to 10 man years of work.

To allow essential initial enhancement and to guarantee subsequent routine updating of their primary SMR databases, we recommend that the parent bodies of county and National Park SMRs should:

- in consultation with the RCHME and EH initiate audits of the current condition of their SMRs and prepare costed specifications for the enhancement of those records by the year 2000/1 to the standard required for effective implementation of the GDO and PPG 16;
- plan to support one or more full-time members of staff responsible for completion and enhancement of the primary SMR database during all or part of the period 1993/4–2000/1;
- in addition to the above, undertake to support a minimum half-post permanently responsible for the updating of the SMR database in the light of new research and discoveries.

The enhancement of SMRs so that they are fully consistent with national data standards is a national requirement. The work of enhancement commenced through the *This Common Inheritance* initiative will need to be continued to ensure that SMRs are fully consistent with national needs. We recommend that the DNH provides funding for this in advance of local government reorganisation.

6

THE FUTURE ORGANISATION, SCOPE AND CONTENT OF THE EXTENDED NATIONAL RECORD

6·1

THE EXTENDED NATIONAL RECORD

Central to the concept of the extended national database is the maintenance of a national index of all buildings, sites and ancient monuments of archaeological, architectural and historical interest in England and its territorial waters. In this index a core record for each building, site or ancient monument should include information on location, type, date, condition, legal status, related interventions and references to principal sources of information. It is this core record that will provide the essential link between the unified NMR and SMRs together with other related records such as those of EH and the DNH relating to scheduled monuments and listed buildings.

6·2

ACCESS TO THE EXTENDED NATIONAL RECORD

The current programme of data exchange between the RCHME and SMRs is effectively creating core records for all sites in the extended national record. If, as is recommended below, SMRs become responsible for updating the record through literature search at a local level, then it will be necessary for the existing protocols for data exchange to be reviewed, so that this information would be available nationally.

At present the extended archaeological national record will only be accessible in its totality through the unified NMR. The RCHME will be examining how this record is best made available on-line to SMRs and EH. It would also be theoretically possible for SMRs to be part of the unified NMR network. Four SMRs are already using the NAR data as the basis of a new SMR, running on software almost identical to that used for the NAR, while a further three are using the same system but with data transferred from an earlier SMR system. Proposals experimentally to link the Lancashire SMR to the unified NMR are included in the RCHME Corporate Plan for 1993/4.

In the course of our present survey thirty-two SMRs confirmed that they were interested in the principle of a networked national heritage information system, although many had reservations about:

- ❖ the cost of its development and maintenance;
- ❖ its relevance to the work of local SMRs;
- ❖ control of access to confidential and sensitive information;
- ❖ control of the use and charging of copyright information.

Interest has already been expressed by EH in linking the computerised record of scheduled monuments in England to the archaeological information in the unified NMR. We recommend that the RCHME and EH proceed to network these records, partly to demonstrate the value of data networking for other areas where decisions still remain to be taken.

It should be noted that the Royal Commission on Ancient and Historical Monuments (Wales) is already moving towards the provision of a networked national archaeological record, linking the Commission's records to those of the five SMRs in Wales.

6.3

NMR RESPONSIBILITY FOR THE ENHANCEMENT OF THE EXTENDED RECORD

ARCHAEOLOGICAL SITES AND LANDSCAPES

The Royal Commission's current Strategic and Corporate Plan *(Corporate Plan, 1989/90–1995/6)* confirms that an increased proportion of the core resources of its Archaeology Division will henceforth be devoted to enhancement and updating of the primary national record of archaeological sites. From the outset, special attention will be given to ensuring that the record is extended to include all significant sites up to a new terminal date of 1945. This will be achieved through parallel programmes of in-house and contracted-out field investigation, air photographic transcription, documentary recording and data exchange carried out to a standard level and specification (RCHME 1992a; RCHME 1992b).

MARITIME SITES

In parallel with its programme of terrestrial recording, the NAR is committed to the rapid development of a record of archaeological sites and wrecks in territorial waters around the coast of England. Following the completion of a joint pilot project with the Hampshire and Isle of Wight county SMRs, the RCHME intends to initiate further recording projects in other maritime counties, with the aim of achieving national coverage by 1995. The RCHME recommends that all maritime recording be co-ordinated by its own specialist staff, and that SMRs planning to develop maritime recording programmes should liaise closely with the RCHME.

HISTORIC BUILDINGS

Since 1985 the Royal Commission and English Heritage have been seeking funds for the systematic computerisation of the DoE 'Greenback' lists of statutorily protected historic buildings. Following the completion of a marketing and feasibility study (Pannell Kerr Forster Associates 1990) and of pilot projects in County Durham and Derbyshire, the RCHME hopes to initiate a national programme of computerised recording in 1993/4. The results of this exercise will provide the core of the national computerised record of historic buildings.

HIGHER LEVEL ARCHAEOLOGICAL AND ARCHITECTURAL RECORDING

In addition to its programmes of primary archaeological and architectural recording the Royal Commission will continue to devote resources and expertise to more intensive recording, the results of which will be automatically included within the NMR.

Within the Archaeology Division future programmes will include:

❖ field survey of monuments and areas of outstanding archaeological interest for the selective enhancement of the national record and to provide information for inclusion on Ordnance Survey maps, and for use by other government agencies;
❖ field survey documentary and air photographic transcription required by SMRs, English Heritage and other external clients for archaeological preservation and management;
❖ enhancement of the national index of archaeological excavations and other archaeological fieldwork;
❖ cataloguing of archaeological archives and collections held within the NAR and elsewhere;
❖ aerial reconnaissance and photography by the RCHME Air Photography Unit and RCHME-funded regional air photographers.

Within the Architectural Division there will be the combination of the following activities:

- ❖ the emergency recording of buildings threatened with partial or total demolition;
- ❖ project recording focusing on specific building types of national significance, eg, hospitals and farmsteads;
- ❖ the cataloguing of architectural records, comprising in-house and deposited reports, drawings, photographs and other collections.

In all of its recording initiatives the Royal Commission will be seeking to maximise the use of its existing base of specialist skills and experience. As well as ensuring the highest possible standard of training for its own permanent and temporary staff, it intends to devote a larger proportion of its resources to the training and guidance of the staff of local authority SMRs, archaeological units and independent practices.

The RCHME is also aware that compatible development of the newly unified NMR and SMRs will depend on much greater consistency in the way in which architectural and archaeological records are compiled. In addition to co-ordinating the development of new national information and data standards the RCHME intends to assist in the promotion of technical and academic standards for the recording of archaeological sites and historic buildings.

Guidelines for the recording of standing buildings have already been published (RCHME 1991a) and comparable documents covering archaeological earthwork and air photographic survey are in preparation. In each case, the specification distinguishes alternative methods and levels of recording that may be applied to a standing building or archaeological site. Henceforth, the quality and depth of all NMR monument accounts and descriptions will be explicitly defined in terms of these levels of recording.

6.4 SMR RESPONSIBILITY FOR THE ENHANCEMENT OF THE EXTENDED RECORD

The creation and updating of records at present remains divided between the NAR and individual SMRs. We recommend that the task of creating and maintaining the primary archaeological record should in future fall in part to local SMRs on grounds of their specialised local knowledge, experience and contacts. Inevitably, detailed arrangements and delegations will depend on the current availability of skills and resources within SMRs or amongst independent subcontractors. In broad terms, however, it is recommended that SMRs should be responsible for primary recording, to nationally agreed standards, of information acquired from:

- ❖ locally published books and journals;
- ❖ local museums and record offices;
- ❖ unpublished local fieldwork, oral reports and chance finds;
- ❖ air photographs.

This does not impinge on the discretion of local authorities to enhance their SMRs in response to local need. The depth of field investigation or documentary research carried out by an SMR or on its behalf will depend on the purpose of the investigation, although it is desirable that subsequent SMR recording should whenever possible conform to nationally agreed standards.

A critical concern to both the RCHME and English Heritage is that any enhancement of SMR records should be of a quality and consistency that meets both local and national requirements. This will only be achieved if recording is carried out by well-trained staff and subject to stringent quality control procedures.

The Royal Commission recognises that the task of completing the primary national record of archaeological sites must be one of collaboration between the NMR and individual local SMRs.

6·5
RCHME SUPPORT FOR SMR ENHANCEMENT

While arguing that the maintenance of an established SMR record is the responsibility of the local authority or other parent body, the RCHME acknowledges that the completion and subsequent updating of the core national record of the historic environment is a task that it should share with SMR parent bodies on an equal basis. During 1992/3 the RCHME will have devoted the equivalent of £0·39m to its programme of combined NMR–SMR primary recording and enhancement. Depending on the continued availability of funds from its own parent body, the Department of National Heritage, the RCHME intends over the nine-year period 1992/3–2000/1 to make further contributions through:

- grant aid to SMRs for the completion of qualitative audits of their current records;
- the contracting through SMRs or other approved agents of additional field, documentary or air photographic recording required to bring the current SMR record to a nationally agreed minimum level of breadth and quality;
- the commitment of an increased proportion of its own in-house staff resource to primary archaeological recording on behalf of both the NMR and the local SMRs.

In the period 1993/4–1995/6 the annual value of this contribution is planned at £0·4m, of which a rising proportion is expected to be applied in the form of external contract and grant aid. In the remaining years of the decade the RCHME will seek to maintain the level of resource for primary NMR–SMR enhancement at 1992/3 values.

6·6
LOCAL AUTHORITY SUPPORT FOR SMR ENHANCEMENT

To assist local authorities in their forward planning, and as a foundation for detailed discussion and negotiation, the RCHME is concerned to clarify that it will not be prepared to contribute to the core costs of housing and maintaining local SMRs, nor for the costs of providing a local service of archaeological information and advice to meet the requirements of the GDO and PPG 16. These provisions should remain the responsibility of the local authority, whether SMR services are provided as an in-house facility or obtained from elsewhere. The RCHME would thus strongly support the inclusion of the cost of SMR maintenance and enhancement within all future local authority Standard Spending Assessments (SSAs).

6·7
AREAS FOR SMR ENHANCEMENT

The Review has shown that in particular the NMR and SMRs require enhancement for records of:

- sites and monuments of the Industrial Revolution;
- military constructions of the First and Second World Wars;
- archaeological deposits in historic towns and villages;
- plough-levelled sites recorded by air photography;
- archaeological and historic landscapes;
- maritime sites in the offshore and inter-tidal zones;
- historic place-name evidence.

The Review has also identified the need for consistent recording of the form in which the archaeological resource survives. Information in the NAR would enable retrospective entry of data on site survival since 1947. We recommend that the RCHME, ACAO and EH jointly discuss information requirements in this area.

6.8 RCHME SUPPORT FOR DATA STANDARDS WORK

Harmonisation of existing records with the data standards being agreed by the RCHME, ACAO and EH will be essential in the extended national record for information users at a national or regional level. The RCHME will encourage acceptance of these emerging core data standards through the provision of technical assistance, and in appropriate circumstances financial support, for any necessary recasting or structuring of existing computerised records. We recommend that the DNH provides funding for this work in advance of local government reorganisation.

We recommend that the RCHME/ACAO Information Standards Working Party continues to develop and monitor data standards for the extended national record, extending this work to provide standards for the data structure of SMRs.

6.9 STANDARDS FOR CARTOGRAPHIC RECORDS

All SMRs support their textual records with map-based records depicting the location of historically significant sites. The format and quality of these mapped records is nevertheless very varied. In addition, the simultaneous compilation of record maps by SMRs, English Heritage and the Royal Commission involves significant duplication of effort, and has militated against the development of common standards of map depiction. This will in the very near future inhibit the effective exploitation of Geographic Information System technology.

We recommend that the RCHME and ACAO should discuss the need for a review of current mapping conventions and standards with a view to adding this to the areas still to be examined by the RCHME/ACAO Information Standards Working Party.

6.10 GEOGRAPHIC INFORMATION SYSTEMS

The power of GIS lies in its ability to allow different kinds of information to be compared and analysed in terms of geographical location and spatial association. In the near future the use of electronic systems for storing and manipulating map-based information will become essential both for the national monitoring and evaluation of England's stock of historic buildings and archaeological sites and for day-to-day use of heritage information within local SMRs.

In 1987 the Chorley Report (DoE 1987) confirmed the immense potential of GIS technology for industry, government and professional fields concerned with interpretation of spatial data. It also emphasised that the full benefit of GIS would only be reaped if those responsible for assembling different sets of information were prepared to recognise certain core data standards.

In the heritage field, the use of GIS technology has thus far been limited to experimental projects, no national body or SMR having yet committed itself to the implementation of a full-scale GIS programme. However, pressure is now mounting for such decisions to be taken by both the RCHME and EH as part of their developing Information System Strategies, and by individual county SMRs required to incorporate heritage data within the global GIS systems being established by their parent local authorities.

To ensure that these separate ventures do not lead to a proliferation of incompatible geographical data and excessive duplication of effort we recommend:

- ❖ that the RCHME and English Heritage should ensure full harmonisation of their respective development of GIS and other electronic and manual cartographic systems;
- ❖ that the RCHME, RCAHMW and RCAHMS should jointly liaise with the Ordnance Survey to ensure national compatibility in the field of digital mapping;
- ❖ that the ACAO and ADAO, in association with the RCHME, should monitor developments within English county and district local authorities and seek to

identify core data standards that will guarantee compatible geographical and cartographic recording of heritage data across local authority boundaries;
❖ the Association for Geographic Information should be encouraged to promote the harmonised national and international application of GIS and digital mapping technology for archaeological and architectural research and cultural heritage management in Britain.

6·11 COMPUTER SECURITY

Assisted by English Heritage and the RCHME, and with increasing encouragement from their parent bodies, all SMRs have completed or are in the later stages of computerising their primary level textual records. Current arrangements for the security of computer-held data are nevertheless variable. We recommend that the RCHME and other interested bodies should jointly define and publish guidelines for the security of computer-held data, and that adherence to those guidelines should be a condition of (a) recognition of an SMR by the ACAO and ADAO and (b) RCHME or English Heritage grant aid or technical support for SMR computerisation.

6·12 OTHER RELATED ARCHAEOLOGICAL RECORDS

The NMR is responsible for the monitoring, acquisition, copying and curation of any other archives, photographs, drawings and unpublished written accounts of archaeological sites, buildings and other elements of the historic environment deemed to be of importance to the National Archaeological Record, National Buildings Record and National Library of Air Photographs under the terms of a published statement of NMR Collecting Policy (RCHME 1991b). It also provides for the curation of textual, graphical and photographic records created in the course of field survey, documentary research and other forms of investigation carried out by the Royal Commission or on its behalf by external contractors or joint partners. In the future it is also intended that the NMR should, in association with English Heritage, provide an index to all archaeological assessments and evaluations, holding copies where possible.

Alongside a general primary level record, most SMRs contain more detailed records relating to particular classes of monument and areas of interest. These enhanced records have normally resulted from programmes of field investigation, aerial survey and detailed documentary research initiated by the SMR itself or in association with other external partners. The RCHME and ACAO are agreed that SMRs are proper repositories of this deeper level of information, provided that it is documented in a way that allows its ready retrieval on behalf of specialist users.

Local SMRs do not normally possess accommodation suited to the long-term storage of unique archival material (ie to the standards of environmental control recommended by the Public Record Office and county record offices). Moreover, few SMRs are in a position to employ staff formally trained in the curation and conservation of historic paper and photographic records. We recommend that:

❖ all local and special-purpose SMRs should draw up and maintain formal statements of Collecting Policy in line with those adopted by members of the Museums Association, county record offices and the NMR;
❖ SMRs should not normally maintain collections of unique archival items;
❖ unpublished excavation records, photographic negatives and other unique material of local or regional importance should be deposited within an appropriate local museum or record office. In the case of records of national importance, or of collections covering different parts of the country, a more appropriate place of secure deposit would be the NMR.

6·13 COLLECTIONS OF AERIAL PHOTOGRAPHS

All SMRs recognise the value of air photographs as a source of evidence. There is nevertheless significant variation in the size and scope of collections of air photographs maintained by individual SMRs. Some are content to acquire representative examples of photographs from independently managed national and local collections; others, especially those actively involved in aerial reconnaissance, give priority to the maintenance of larger and more extensive collections of their own.

Air photographic collecting policy is properly a matter for agreement between an SMR and its parent body, but requires co-ordination with the Royal Commission's National Library of Air Photographs (NLAP) if excessive duplication of photographic printing, archiving and cataloguing is to be avoided. It is therefore recommended that the RCHME in association with the ACAO and the CBA Aerial Archaeology Committee should:

❖ review current arrangements for the simultaneous archiving of specialist oblique aerial photographs at national and local level;
❖ take steps to ensure compatible cataloguing and referencing of air photographs within the NLAP and local SMR collections.

References

Aberg, F A and Leech, R H 1992. 'The National Archaeological Record for England. Past, present and future' in C U Larsen (ed) *Sites & Monuments National Archaeological Records* (National Museum of Denmark), 157–69

ACAO 1978. *A Guide to the Establishment of Sites and Monuments Records*

ACAO 1991. *Sites and Monuments Records – Access and Charging* (1st edn)

ACAO 1993. *Sites and Monuments Records – Policies for Access and Charging* (2nd edn)

Benson, D 1974. 'A Sites and Monuments Record for the Oxford region'. *Oxoniensia* **37** (1972), 226–37

Burrow, I 1984. 'The history of the Sites and Monuments Record system' in I Burrow (ed) *County Archaeological Records: Progress and Potential* (ACAO), 6–15

Chadburn, A 1989. 'Computerised county Sites and Monuments Records in England: an overview of their structure, development and progress' in S Rahtz and J Richards (eds) *Computer Applications and Quantitative Methods in Archaeology*, BAR International Series 548, 9–18

Clubb, N 1990. 'Computerised county Sites and Monuments Records – technical aspects' in M Hughes (ed) *Sites and Monuments Records: Some Current Issues* (ACAO), unpaginated

Coopers & Lybrand Deloitte 1990. *Marketing Strategy for the NMR* (unpublished report to the RCHME)

Council of Europe 1990. 'Council Directive of 7 June 1990 on freedom of access to information on the environment'. *Official Journal of the European Communities*, 23 June 1990, No. L 158/56–58

Council of Europe 1991. *Draft Revised Convention on the Protection of the Archaeological Heritage*

Countryside Commission 1991. *Fit for the Future*

DoE 1972. *Field Monuments and Local Authorities*, Circular 11/72

DoE 1984. *England's Archaeological Resource: A Rapid Quantification of the National Archaeological Resource and a Comparison with the Schedule of Ancient Monuments*

DoE 1986. *The Town and Country Planning General Development Order 1988*

DoE 1987. *Handling Geographical Information: Report of the Committee of Enquiry Chaired by Lord Chorley*

DoE 1990a. *This Common Inheritance*

DoE 1990b. *Policy and Planning Guidance Note 16: Archaeology and Planning*

English Heritage 1991. *Exploring our Past: Strategies for the Archaeology of England*

Fraser, D 1984. 'Sites and Monuments Records: the state of the art' in I Burrow (ed) *County Archaeological Records: Progress and Potential* (ACAO), 47–55

Hart, J and Leech, R H 1989. 'The National Archaeological Record' in S Rahtz and J Richards (eds) *Computer Applications and Quantitative Methods in Archaeology*, BAR International Series 548, 57–67

KPMG Peat Marwick McLintock 1988. *The Royal Commissions on Ancient and Historic Monuments in England, Scotland and Wales* (unpublished report to the DoE)

Lang, N 1990. 'Sites and Monuments Records: some current issues' in M Hughes (ed) *Sites and Monuments Records: Some Current Issues* (ACAO), unpaginated

Oracle UK Ltd 1990. *RCHME Information Systems Strategy Study* (unpublished report to the RCHME)

Pagoda Associates 1992. *An Evaluation of the Impact of PPG 16 on Archaeology and Planning* (unpublished report to English Heritage)

Pannell Kerr Forster Associates 1990. *Project Landmarks: A Report on the Marketability of Computerised Listed Buildings Records* (unpublished report to the RCHME, EH and DoE)

Phillips, C W 1980. Chapters 24 and 23 (part) in W A Seymour (ed) *A History of the Ordnance Survey*

RCHME 1990a. 'RCHME lead role for SMRs'. *British Archaeological News* **5**, 23

RCHME 1990b. *National Monuments Record: A Guide to the Archive*

RCHME 1991a. *Recording Historic Buildings: A Descriptive Specification* (2nd edn)

RCHME 1991b. *Collecting Policy*

RCHME 1992a. *The Archaeological Field Survey Programme, 1992/3–1996/7* (unpublished consultation document)

RCHME 1992b. *The National Air Photographic Mapping Programme* (unpublished consultation document)

RCHME and English Heritage 1989. *Revised Thesaurus of Architectural Terms*

RCHME and English Heritage 1992. *Thesaurus of Archaeological Site Types* (2nd edn)

Serpell, D 1979. *Report of the Ordnance Survey Review Committee*

Walsh, D 1969. *Report of the Committee of Enquiry into the Arrangements for the Protection of Field Monuments (1966–8)*

Spotlight on
The Night Sky

Tim Wood

Franklin Watts
London · New York · Sydney · Toronto

© 1988 Franklin Watts

Franklin Watts
12a Golden Square
London W1

Franklin Watts Australia
14 Mars Road
Lane Cove
NSW 2066

Phototypeset by Keyspools Limited
Printed in Hong Kong

UK ISBN: 0 86313 689 3
US ISBN: 0–531–10545–8
Library of Congress Catalog Card Number: 87–51478

Illustrations:
Russell Barnett
Hayward Art Group
Hayward and Martin
Michael Roffe

Photographs:
NASA
Space Frontiers Ltd
ZEFA

Design:
Janet King
David Jefferis

Technical Consultant:
Iain Nicholson BSc, FRAS

Note: A number of the illustrations in this book originally appeared in *The Night Sky*, An Easy-Read Fact Book.